IF I SHOULD DIE BEFORE I LIVE

KEN JONES

ISBN E-book edition: ISBN Print edition:ISBN-13: 978-1-7321487-0-3

For other resources, please visit: ken jones.direct

❀ Created with Vellum

FOREWORD

I first met Ken many years ago at a writing conference where I was the teacher and he was a student. Boy, did I have that wrong. For one thing, Ken seems to effortlessly put down one perfect sentence after another, rolling out stories that fire your imagination, and regularly delivering profound insights like the nationally recognized author that he is. For another, he became for me the kind of wise friend and teacher every man hopes to find at least once in his life.

Ken is both a pastor and a personal life development coach for high-achieving professionals—people who clearly know how to master time or they wouldn't have all those letters after their names and live in such big houses. Then again, maybe not, because they invest their valuable time and resources coaching with Ken. A coach, he says, is someone who helps people focus on and move toward what matters most, and he works hard at living by his own advice. "Each morning when the sun comes up," he writes, "I pray it dawns on me all over again: a new appreciation for the journey, a new understanding of the God who gives me life, the God who inhabits eternity."

In *If I Should Die Before I Live,* Ken Jones helps us make sure we're not missing our own life. (Talk about what matters most.) He wants us to know at the end of every day that we're actually "living life in the midst of our *daze.*"

As smart people like Einstein, C. S. Lewis and Charlie Brown knew, time routinely fools us. (The writer of Ecclesiastes blamed it on a kind of clock-less void in our hearts that he called eternity.) We routinely think we have all the time in the world. We pour endless energy into regretting the past or fretting about the future, all the while missing the only *now* that's ours to live. We think we've got things figured; we think we're keeping careful track of time. But one day we turn around to find that a cherished dream or the love of our life or a whole era has slipped away on us. And we find ourselves pleading with the psalmist, "Lord, teach me to number my days."

I began reading Ken's book in an apartment in New York City, where my wife, Heather, and I had lived for three years. I continued reading and taking notes as my son and I drove across Utah in a moving truck. I finished it in a coffee shop in Oregon. I needed Ken's book. I was leaving behind the familiar, and moving toward something else, a new future, but a future of what? What mattered most now? How should I number my days now? I have found in his wry, kindly voice in the pages that follow exactly the kind of mentoring I needed. I know you will too.

Think of the book you're holding as the pink slip you've been waiting for, the hall pass for your own personal great escape from that awful droning sound of an unconsidered life. Lucky you.

My advice is grab Ken's offer of freedom and don't let go. You'll be so glad you did.

David Kopp

Editor, author; formerly executive editor, vice president, Convergent Books

INTRODUCTION

"When I reach the end of my days, a moment or two from now, I must look backward on something more meaningful than the pursuit of houses and land, and stocks and bonds. I will consider my earthly existence to have been wasted unless I can recall a loving family, a consistent investment in the lives of people, and an earnest attempt to serve the God who made me. Nothing else makes much sense."

(Dr. James Dobson's "Family Talk")

"What I fear now is that I will somehow miss what it is that I am supposed to learn here, something important enough that the Dreamer dispatched me, and the rest of us, here to learn. What I fear now is that I will somehow miss the point of living here at all, living here between the dreaming and the coming true."

(Robert Benson, in "Between the Dreaming and the Coming True")

If you came home this evening, and one of your family members were to ask you, "How was your day?" what would your response be?

"Good. It was a good day."

Or, if it's been particularly stressful, chaotic, or ridiculously busy, would you respond with an answer like,

"Interesting,"

or

"Challenging,"

or

"Tiring,"

or

"Ridiculous."

I'm relatively sure you *wouldn't* respond with a question of your own. You wouldn't answer by asking, "Which day are you talking about?" You would assume the day you were being asked about was Today. And without even thinking, you might begin to describe Today.

But what of the 'other' days we've been assigned to navigate? There are six additional days that contain the life God had in mind, when He thought of all of us. This little book is about the totality of all those days.

The days?

The names of all our days are these:

- Someday
- Any Day
- Every Day
- Yesterday
- Today
- Tomorrow
- A Day of Rest

These God-created days represent pockets of time, each containing a uniqueness all its own, filled with divinely important truths along the paths of daily living. Occasions and relationships, challenges and opportunities. Day after day, as if we were on some giant merry-go-round, each of us rides the up-and-down of life's tempo and drama. Sun up. Sun down. Life "comes to pass" on a daily basis.

But, it doesn't come to stay.

This is a book about our God-ordained days: the seven ordinary and extraordinary epochs of time God graciously granted all of us to live; days every living soul must become acquainted with, and navigate, and understand. It's a book about reflecting on our moments; keeping track of our days, living life in the midst of our *daze*, trusting God to help us manage our days. If you're like me, (and I know that, at least in some important ways, you are) you've lived through these seven days many times. The question is not, 'Did we live through them,' but rather, 'What did we *learn* in the process of surviving them?'

Time is a non-renewable resource. God only made so many moments for each of us to live. When the number of my days is completed, what comes after that will be eternally significant.

So, if today has been particularly challenging, or hectic, or frustrating, or just plain ridiculously busy? Take time. Slow down. Yes. Sit down, and invest some of the moments God has granted you to read through this little book. Who knows?

You may find answers to things you've always wondered about.

Or, you may decide to finally address for yourself that pesky 'What if?' question.

You know the one I mean?

"What if I should die ... before I live?"

Kj

THE FIRST DAY

S omeday ... For Dreaming

"Rivers know this: there is no hurry. We shall get there some day."

— POOH'S LITTLE INSTRUCTION BOOK, INSPIRED BY A. A.
MILNE

ONCE, I heard a story about a missionary who went to a far off island to tell the people there about God. He stayed for several years, teaching the people, loving the people, but never leaving the island. Life at times was very lonely for the man. But even though he saw little outward result from his labor, he stayed at his post, and remained faithful to his task.

One day, one of the men of the island came to the missionary with a gift: a seashell of such exquisite color and shape and form that the missionary could hardly believe its beauty. "Where," asked the missionary, "did you find such a wonderful shell? I have lived here on the island for many years, and I have never seen such an incredible thing." The man replied, in his broken English, "Such shells only on far side of island, two days walk from here, hidden in cove, hard to find."

Such a touching expression humbled the missionary, and he thanked his friend. "I appreciate your beautiful gift, but you really shouldn't have gone to such incredible trouble. You had to walk such a long distance to find it."

And the man said, "Long walk is part of gift."

And so it is...with Someday.

It is because God is a good God, I think, that He allowed a day like Someday to be included in our lives. Of all the days we will ever have to experience or deal with, Someday is perhaps the most complex. Someday possesses an almost magical power to help us dream, and hope and wait. It prompts us to envision things we might otherwise never be able to imagine. The things we dream about, the things we long for, and hope for and envision? They aren't here yet. But we trust they will be ... Someday.

In some ways, Someday is remote, detached from the present, and far away. Someday sets off in the distance, like the glow of an evening sun. It casts an illusory shadow, easy to see but hard to hold in our hands. The comfort of Someday can be as real as the warmth of a fire in a wood stove on a cold winter night. The consolation we receive from believing that Someday things can be different represents a very real promise for the future. Perhaps it is because we understand *that* reality that we also assume something else: We don't know exactly when Someday will be here, but it feels as if it is a very long walk from "*now.*"

One of the things I've noticed about Someday is how much

there is to "do" there. Someday is the day we'll retire, of course. But it's also the day we'll build our dream house, or finally get some grandkids. Someday we'll write a book, or take a trip, or finish our education. Someday, our troubles will seem like a bump in the road.

Someday, Christian people believe, we'll get to go to heaven. But, that hope also carries with it a certain dread that is equally true of Someday. In addition to a faith in Christ, in order to go to heaven, we have to die. And most of us have determined to postpone that eventuality for as long as possible. We all know that Someday we'll die, but not right away, thank you.

Someday also represents opportunity; a chance for change, and a window through which we see and imagine. The limitless possibilities of Someday can transport us beyond the pain and numbness of whatever unpleasant circumstance we might currently find ourselves. If God had created time without including Someday, we would be doomed to the discouragements of life *now*, and lose our desire to go on.

Paul told the Romans that, "... hope does not disappoint us." (Rom. 5:5) It's when we lose hope in Someday that we stop searching for solutions. In fact, one of the greatest reasons people give up on relationships, or some of the things they may have worked for most of their lives, is that they've lost their ability to dream, to envision, to hope for a better day. When we lose our ability to imagine that life will ever be any different than it is right now, we've denied ourselves the opportunities that can only be found ... Someday.

I would not for a moment try to paint a picture of Someday as a panacea or Shangri-La. In some ways, hoping to live a fulfilled life Someday is like running after a bus we can't quite catch that's on its way to a place we'd love to visit. No matter how fast we run, Someday continues to stay ahead of us. We long for rest from the journey. Won't life be better, Someday? Won't the picture be clearer, Someday? Everyone who's lived much of life at all knows that the answer to those questions is, "Not necessarily." (Perhaps, but not necessarily.)

Expectation and disappointment love to walk hand-in-hand throughout life, twin images reversed in the mirror of life's reflection. I know that it is so. Someday can seem to have such promise. Yet, like a fickle trickster, it is not above making promises it cannot keep.

I have known that truth since I was in the fifth grade.

I BELIEVE it was in the fifth grade that I first became aware of Someday. When I was in the fifth grade, my teacher was Miss Graham. I started playing the trumpet that year in the school band. (My dad told me that if I practiced, Someday I'd be as good as Harry James.) I took a growth spurt that year too, and almost caught up with Debbie Swenson, the tallest girl in our class. Almost, but not quite. My mom kept telling me that Someday I'd be as tall as Debbie. (I haven't seen Debbie in more than forty years, so I'm not sure that ever happened.)

We had a fifth-grade spelling bee, too. Our class competed against the other fifth-grade class, I suppose to see which teacher could teach spelling the best. I was almost the last kid still standing at the end of that competition.

Almost, but not quite.

Miss Graham gave me too hard a word right near the end, and I had to sit down. I was close, though. In fact, I really only missed one letter in my word. I spelled *elephant* with an "f" and didn't know why I had missed it until I got back to my seat. Margaret Anne Murphey (who, by the way, had already taken her seat on the word *illustrate* because she didn't know it had double *l*'s) looked at me like I was some kind of dumb nut. I still remember her words as I slinked down at my desk. I can still see her face, hear that expression in her voice.

"Don't you know there's no "*f*" in *elephant?*" she said.

I told her that, no, I hadn't realized there was no "*f*" in *elephant,* but that I did know about the double *l* in *illustrate,* and that I had known *that* word since way back in fourth grade.

I learned a lot that year, sitting in the back row. Most of the time I tried to listen while Miss Graham taught, but occasionally, like a lot of the kids in my class I suspect, I looked out of those huge windows in our classroom and daydreamed about a time when things would be different. I longed for Someday.

I could hardly wait to grow up when I was a kid. I remember telling my mom once that I wished I was a grown-up already, and she told me not to wish my life away.

But I did.

"Someday" filled my thoughts when I was in the fifth grade. I dreamed of what life would be like Someday, when I was in the seventh grade. Seventh graders in my hometown all went to one school downtown called Central Junior High. They got to ride the bus to school; they didn't have to walk to school like mere children. I envied those kids who got to ride a school bus to school when I was in the fifth grade. I wondered what it would be like to move from class to class every day, too. Seventh-graders don't have to stay put. Every hour, a bell rings and they get to move to a different class and teacher; seventh-graders get to see a whole different group of kids every hour. But, in the fifth-grade, Miss Graham didn't even reassign our seats for the entire year, and my only worldview, day-in and day-out, was the back of Margaret Anne Murphey's head. Our bell only rang twice a day: once at the beginning of the day to let the teacher know how many kids were tardy, and once at the end of the day, so the teacher would know she didn't have to hold us prisoner any longer.

I still remember how I envied those lucky-dog-seventh-graders when I was in the fifth-grade. I knew that Someday, I'd get to enjoy the good life of the seventh-grade, too.

Or at least that's what I thought.

But, you know what? When I got to the seventh-grade, it wasn't anything like I had imagined. It's true that I didn't have to endure the humiliation of those childish fifth-grade spelling bees, but I did have to write essays on stuff like the American Revolution and the difference between Democrats and Republicans. And, while it was true that all of the grade schools in my hometown sent their seventh-graders to Central Junior High, some of the kids at Central were from "across the tracks," and turned out to be meaner than snakes. They'd just as soon beat you up as look at you. No, although I dreamed about how cool life would be Someday in the seventh-grade, by the time I got there, it really wasn't that great. I never gave up, though. No matter what grade I was in, or what stage of life I found myself, I still kept thinking and waiting ... for Someday.

Someday, I'd get to go to high school, and drive a car, and play on the football team and (gulp!) date girls. However, in all my dreaming about Someday, I somehow neglected the reality that Someday I would also have acne, and get cut from the football squad, and have trouble finding a date. It's true that Someday, wonderful things would come into my life. I would go to college, and get married, and buy a house, and have kids. But, it's also true that Someday, loans for my education would come due, and my house would need a new roof, and my kids would need braces. In all my thinking and dreaming about how good life was going to be Someday, I somehow missed the truth that merely enduring life until Someday rolls around had the potential for robbing me of enjoying life "in the moment," or "life in the meantime."

A life resting on a foundation of Someday's uncertainties

wobbles along like it's balanced on a three-legged stool, precarious, and fragile, besides. It would have been nice if I could have grown out of the habit of living life for Someday. But I'm not sure I ever did. On certain days, I still catch myself looking out of the picture window of life's classroom, enchanted by the allure of Someday.

I know. Our ability to imagine the way life could be at some distant point in time is a gift God himself has given us. After all, wasn't it God who gave dreams to Joseph in his multi-colored coat? Didn't God show Joseph some secrets about his older brothers, and the way it would be ... Someday? Didn't He show the future to Isaiah, the prophet and tell him to write it down? God is the one who showed the Apostle John an incredible vision of Someday, when this world would end, as he gave him the Revelation on the Isle of Patmos. The Lord Jesus himself had Someday in mind when He promised to go and prepare a place for us, so that, Someday — after all the other days have come and gone — we could be with Him forever. There's no question that Someday in the hands of the Creator of Heaven and Earth is an awesome thing.

It's the Somedays that have their origins in the minds and hearts of *mere men* that don't always pan out. In a word: Someday isn't always all it's cracked-up to be. Life is unpredictable. When God arranged all our days, he didn't string them in a straight line from point A to point B. He made a circuitous design, serpentine and crooked as a dog's hind leg. Bends and turns in the road of life make it difficult, if not impossible to anticipate what's coming next. And that's where the rub comes.

It's difficult to *anticipate* what actually shows up when what we thought was the distant future finally gets here, but it's not difficult to *imagine* it. Because we are vulnerable to great expectations, we are equally susceptible to bitter disappointments. They go hand in hand. We need to be on our guard, because we can never know when impatience about some Someday in our lives might walk over and pull up a chair. Discontentment with "life in the meantime" may drop by for an unexpected visit, and whisper in our inner ear, "The only day life will ever be any better is Someday. And that's a long, long time from *now*." Or perhaps even worse, we may, like Job of old, lose our ability to imagine that life Someday will ever be any better than it is right now; it might, God forbid, even get worse.

Almost everyone knows about Job, who was minding his own business, trying to serve God, living a good life. But then the "unexpected" showed up, and overwhelmed him. During one particularly difficult session of his suffering, he complained that God "carries out his decree against me, and many such plans *he still has in store*." (Job 23:14, italics added). What Job was really saying was, "*Someday* came to pass, and it wasn't a dream; it was a nightmare. And God's not finished with me yet."

I know of no greater recipe for disillusionment and fatigue of soul and spirit than to live life waiting for Someday to roll around while being discontent in the meantime, or imagining that in that far-off Someday, things will never be any better than the awful way they are right now. For some people, Someday is a nice place to visit. Dreams flourish there. Fulfillment seems to ooze from every moment we allow our minds to spend there. God was good to let us dream about Someday.

But sometimes, there can be a great disparity between the dreaming ... and the coming true.

I will tell you what I mean.

⁓

WE HAVE THREE SONS. If you're a parent, you already know that the day a child is born, dreams for that new life are birthed, as well. I still remember looking into my newborn son's face for the first time. Who would he grow-up to be? Where would he go to college? Who would he marry? A million questions raced around my one-track-mind the day our first child was born. At that moment in time, he was the center of my universe.

Imaginings and supposings are wonderful things. They allow us to savor all the hopes and potentials for the Somedays of our lives. In other words, when we think about Someday, what we're really doing is dreaming.

One of the great things about dreams is that at the moment they are experienced, dreams are real; as real as anything we've ever imagined. And, the day our first son was born, my wife and I had a real dream for his life. Suppose he became a brain surgeon or discovered a cure for cancer? He could possibly become a writer, or an attorney, or an executive. Endless potential stared back at me that very first day I looked into the face of my son for that very first time. I remember praying for him, and already becoming anxious and impatient for the day he could talk to me. *Someday*, I thought. *Someday, you'll be able to play catch with me, and talk to me about baseball, and laugh with me. Someday, we will be great friends.*

And, we are very good friends, my son and I.

I don't know exactly when it happened. But, early in my son's life, one of the dreams I had for *him* was directly related to a dream I had for *me*. Someday, I wanted to be a grandpa, and if that were to ever happen, I would obviously need his cooperation.

I think I've known for a long time that Someday, my wife would make a fabulous grandmother. I've also known that my wife is married to an extraordinary grandpa. Someday I would prove it. It took more than thirty-three years. But, eventually, my long wait ended. Our oldest son and his wife became the parents of Addison Grace, our very first grandchild. I've never been as thrilled with anything in all my life as I am with being a grandpa. Being a grandpa is everything I thought it would be.

And ... being a grandpa is *nothing* like I expected.

The Someday I became a grandpa happened this way. One evening as my wife and I were at home, (and after waiting nine of the longest months we'd ever spent,) we got a nervous and excited call from our son, saying he was taking our daughter-in-law to the hospital. Actually, he said, "Dad, I think this is it."

And so it was. Jennifer was having our grandbaby. My wife and I immediately left our home in Northern California, driving through the night and into the early morning so we could arrive in Los Angeles where they lived. We wanted to be there in time for the birth of our grandchild.

I've been a pastor for a long time, and my wife and I have been on the waiting-room-end of a lot of new babies. We've spent early morning hours with many grandparents, waiting for their blessed events. We've stood at the windows of hospital nurseries with so many families, watching as nurses washed and dressed newborn infants, fresh from their mother's womb. We've celebrated with a lot of other grandparents, believing that Someday, our turn would come.

And it finally did.

After several hours of labor, our daughter-in-law gave birth to Addison Grace. I stood, alongside my wife and other family members, waiting at the hospital nursery window, waiting for our baby to make her incredible entrance. We waited for the nurses to bring her out so we could get a good look at her. We knew she would need to be weighed. She would need to be measured, and washed, and dressed. We had seen it all before, and we knew how the routine should work. We knew that if things went according to plan, the doors to the nursery would soon swing open and some nurse we didn't know would hold up a baby we had never met. She would bring our baby close to the window so we could make a fuss, and say the things new grand-parents are suppose to say at times like this: "She looks like her mother," or "She has lots of hair, doesn't she?" or "Isn't she beautiful? Look at those tiny hands." I had the new digital camera I bought just for this occasion turned on and ready to fire. I didn't want to miss one moment of the excitement.

But, moments have a way of taking a long time when you're waiting for Someday, and this Kodak moment was taking longer to develop than I had anticipated.

I decided to turn the camera off. I didn't want to deplete the batteries when there wasn't anything to take a picture of yet. And the nail-biting minutes of waiting grew into a gnawing concern. Why were they taking so long? Why, after waiting for thirty-three years and then another nine months, did I have to continue to wait for Someday, when I could look into the face of my grandchild? Why the suspense of seeing my granddaughter? Why didn't they bring her out? Why didn't they wash her, and weigh her, and dress her like they were suppose to? It didn't seem right, somehow? It didn't seem as if things were going according to plan.

That was because ... things were not going according to plan.

After my wife and I stood for more than twenty minutes at the nursery window, our son came to tell us we could stop our waiting. Addison wouldn't be making an appearance just yet. I could put my camera away. He told us the doctors wanted the family to gather in the room where Addison had been delivered. The concern on his face seemed strangely incongruous to the joy of this moment.

"Everything alright?" I asked.

"Let's wait until we're all together in the room," he said.

And so, I waited.

My wife and I, along with the rest of our family, walked down a long hospital hallway toward a rendezvous with Someday. It seemed like a very long walk, and a very short wait, before the doctor — a doctor who delivered the granddaughter I couldn't wait to see — brought us news I would not want to hear; news that did not belong in the midst of my Someday. Our Addison Grace, our granddaughter, our very special child ... was a very special child, indeed. Born with a birth defect in which her esophagus did not connect with her stomach, our little Addie was in extremely critical condition. Only minutes old, they already knew she would need immediate surgery.

And ... doctors suspected that our wonderful, precious, fresh-from-heaven granddaughter was born with Down syndrome.

I'm a storyteller. I've been one most of my life. As a storyteller, I have learned over the years that when we tell our stories, sometimes we need to leave parts untold. Some parts need to be left out because they are boring. Other parts are private. Not secret, mind you. Only private, like certain parts of our bodies which, although common to all beings who are human, are nonetheless not meant for public display. I will not share with you all the details and moments my family and I experienced the day Addison Grace was born. I will not tell you everything about the Someday I became a grandpa, because I would never want to cause pain to my family by sharing private moments; moments perplexing beyond description and impossible to describe, besides.

But I will tell you about the exhilaration I experienced at meeting *her* for the very first time, my wonderful, incredible, beautiful and charming granddaughter, Addison Grace. After we learned of Addie's struggle, and while she was still less than an hour old, my son came into the hallway where I stood waiting, and invited me to join him in the neonatal intensive care unit. I felt honored by the privilege being extended to me by my son, an odd "right of passage" offered from a first-time-dad to a first-time-granddad. Thankfully, there were no other babies in that place. No other parents concerned for desperately ill children, no other tiny miracles created in the image of God who were in need of critical care.

When I opened the door and saw her for that very first time, I didn't have my new camera with me, but I wouldn't need it to document this moment in my life. My mind's eye captured a picture for me that I will never, ever forget. She rested under a warming lamp. Sleepy as a morning's yawn, and pink as the blush of any sunrise. Positively amazing was our Addison Grace. I walked across the room to where she was. I leaned. I bent at the waist and placed my face close to hers for a better look. I hovered over her like the grandpa I was, and my eyes scanned every crack and crevice, and lash and hair. She didn't move a muscle, but dozed like a princess. I was totally captivated by this sleeping beauty. And, although her tiny hands were no bigger than a pair of new dimes, ten tiny fingers wrapped themselves around my very being, and held my heart with no effort at all.

And so it was that I spoke to her for the very first time.

"Hello, Addison Grace," I whispered. "It's me, your grandpa, and I've come to tell you that I love you, and I want to pray for you." She did not open her eyes as I spoke. I chose to believe, however, that she could hear and understand my presence. I believed in my heart that she was not sleeping; only resting her eyes. The poignancy of this, our first meeting, seemed strangely incongruous to me: it was, at one-and-the-same-time, a formal introduction and a pull-up-a-chair-and-sit-down-with-someone-you've-known-all-your-life moment in time. The Someday I dreamed about for so long was finally here, and yet, a new Someday —one I had never imagined for my grand baby— made its first appearance on the horizon of my mind. Imagining the future for the "family Jones" at that moment in time seemed a painful and bewildering challenge. But the joy of looking into her face refused to give way to any uncertainty that might lie ahead. I could hardly contain myself, really. I stared. I marveled. I positively reveled in the wonder of this magical encounter. She was finally here. Here in this moment of time. I could see her, and touch her, and share with her my voice, and my love, and my life. I did not stay long at her crib-side.

But, I did stay long enough to pray.

Not a "Now I lay me down to sleep," prayer. Instead, I prayed a *Someday* prayer. Everyone knows that God has all the time in the world. And, since *eternity* and *forever* belong to Him, as I stood alongside my granddaughter, I offered a prayer to the God of all the Somedays Addison will ever face. With every grain of faith I could muster, I summoned the God Who Inhabits Eternity. For a certainty, I prayed with concern about her future, her critical condition, and the challenges that represent life with Down Syndrome. I asked for health and healing. I asked for strength for my son and my wonderful daughter-in-law. So many uncertainties about Addison's future flooded my thoughts at that moment in time that it was difficult to even know how to pray. So, in my heart, where no nurse or doctor or attendant could ever see, I allowed myself to begin to dream. I dreamed for Addison as I prayed. In the midst of my concern, I anticipated. I imagined all the wonderful times we would have together, Someday. And even though she was only an hour old, I asked God for wonderful moments some distant Someday from *now*, when she could look into my eyes and ask me serious and mysterious questions; questions like, "How did grandpas get so wrinkled?" or, "Why don't cats and dogs like each other?" And, I prayed for the day I could ask her important questions of my own; things like "Would you like a chocolate ice cream cone ... or vanilla?"

I will never forget the day I became a grandpa. It was, indeed, everything I had dreamed it would be, and nothing like I expected. No day I have ever lived can compare to the exhilaration and joy, the surprise and unexpected sorrow I experienced within such a short period of time. As I write these words, our Addison Grace continues to grow and flourish and amaze. She's already learned some of life's greatest skills: how to laugh out loud at her grandpa, and charm her grandpa by holding his hand and loving people, and loving God. She can dance the legs off a June bug, and her smile can melt an iceberg. She is, quite simply, amazing. And I'm grateful the future looks bright for her. Bright, but not easy to anticipate or predict. The protector in me would love to shield her from hurtful things; biting words, insensitive people, and the sorrows every human soul is acquainted with.

But I cannot.

The truth is that the Somedays that await Addison are not unlike the Somedays that await me, the Somedays that await us all. Experience teaches me that a year or two from now, or a month or two from now, or even a moment or two from now, a Someday I never anticipated will again knock on the door of my serene and tranquil life, and I will be obliged to acknowledge its arrival. In other words, some day, Someday will come along again. And, whatever life I may be living at that moment in time will have to make room for the challenges, disappointments, joys and sorrows that have suddenly crowded into another day. The Apostle Paul said we live by faith, not by sight, and I believe it. Someday I'll get to go to heaven because of my faith in Jesus.

But, even heaven can't be fully imagined or anticipated. No eye has seen, no ear has heard, no mind has conceived what God has prepared for those who love him. Someday, if we trust Jesus, we'll *know*. But for now? We *walk*. We follow the course of God's loving, benevolent, sovereign way for each of us, experiencing all the twists and turns of life "in the meantime."

And, life in the meantime ... can be a mean time.

Each morning when the sun comes up, I pray it will dawn on me all over again: a new appreciation for the journey, a new understanding of the God who gives me life, the God who inhabits eternity. On days when life seems weary, or hard, or impossible. On days when the gifts that come my way are positively indescribable in their beauty and complexity, I need to remind myself that the path I walk with God isn't predictable, and it certainly isn't easy. It's just that you can't get to the end of the mystery of life without walking through the pages of the dramatic story God had in mind when he thought of you.

And, that long walk that we make as we trust and follow God? That long walk is part of the gift ... of Someday.

2

THE SECOND DAY

A ny Day (now) ... For waiting

"It's not that I'm afraid to die; I just don't want to be there when it happens."

"I live now on borrowed time, waiting in the anteroom for the summons that will inevitably come."

"Thith ith taking too long.

— WOODY ALLEN, AGATHA CHRISTIE, SIMEON JONES
(AGE 4), WHILE WAITING FOR ICE CREAM

If you ever get to come to my house to visit, you'll notice something as soon as you walk in the door. My wife has a thing about *time*. Actually, she doesn't have a thing about *time*, I guess; she has a thing about *clocks*. She decorated one of the walls of our living room with clocks and timepieces of all sizes and shapes. One clock is a round-faced clock with blue numbers. We got it while on a trip down to Monterey. And, there's a wooden cuckoo clock hanging over on the far right, too. We bought it on a trip several years ago in Germany. It hangs next to a shadow box my wife thought would look nice on her wall of time; a shadow box with several pocket and wrist watches inside. One of the clocks on our wall could easily double as the head of a bass drum if it didn't have numbers and hands on it. It's huge. About the diameter of a wash tub.

When you sit down in our living room, you won't have any trouble at all 'seeing' the time. In fact, you'll have more 'times' than you know what to do with. There must be fifteen different clocks and watches on my wife's wall of time. But, even though you won't have a difficult time finding a clock in our living room, unless you're wearing a watch of your own, you still may have an issue with 'seeing' the correct time. Some of the clocks run a bit fast. Some of them run slower than they should, probably because it's time for me to change the batteries. And some of the clocks on our wall of time have stopped working all together. (We haven't heard a peep out of our cuckoo in so long that I'm not even sure he's still behind that little door.)

No, the fact that a clock *shows* me a time doesn't necessarily mean I am actually *seeing* the time. And, even though I may be wearing a $500 watch that *keeps* perfect time, everyone knows that there is no such thing as 'keeping' time.

And ... everyone knows that "knowing" the correct time is not the same as *realizing* how short time really is, either.

THERE'S no question that Any Day bears a faint and yet undeni-able family resemblance to Someday. Both days are filled with events and activities we haven't experienced yet. However, Any Day is closer to this very moment in time than Someday. Have you noticed? In fact, Any Day is so close to this very moment in time that we often refer to it as Any Day (*now.*)

And, Any Day is often comprised of even shorter, specific and yet, still-to-be-determined moments or measures of time: Any Minute, (now) and Any Second, (now.)

There is a huge 'time' difference between Someday and Any Day. For example, there's a certain 'ultimacy' or arrival point we can attach to Someday. Most of us believe that, eventually, whatever is going to happen Someday will finally come to pass. We have to wait around for Someday to show up. But, Any Day comes to pass a lot *sooner* than Someday. Any Day always happens 'before long.' There's a certain urgency or immediacy or 'very-soon-ness' we associate with Any Day. In fact, perhaps the easiest way to differentiate between Someday and Any Day might be to think about the difference between your doctor telling you you're going to die Someday, and his telling you you're going to die ... Any Day.

When I'm waiting for a package, or expecting a phone call, or interviewing for a new job, or trying to sell my house, I don't want those unresolved issues to be settled Someday. I want an answer as soon as possible: Any Day (now,) or any minute now, or any second now.

Any Day is the day patience waits for, and perseverance refuses to give up on. So much of life is spent waiting, standing in line, enduring the commercials so the story can continue, or the game can go on.

Waiting, of course, is as common as the tick of a clock. Waiting and developing patience represent some of the most important things human beings can ever engage in. In fact, it is impossible to develop patience without spending a significant amount of time living life Any Day (now.) As you read these words, no matter who you are, or where you are at this moment in time, — you are waiting for something to happen, or resolve itself. Everybody waits. In fact, even God, (who created time, and is so big He doesn't really have to wait for anything if He doesn't want to,) once waited around for something to happen, Any Day (now.) The Apostle Peter, in his first letter mentions that "… God waited patiently in the days of Noah while the ark was being built." (1 Peter 3:20, NIV) I've heard preachers talk about all the ridicule Noah must have endured from his neighbors, as they walked by every day, watching him build that big boat. But, I don't think I've ever heard anyone mention what it must have been like for Noah, knowing that God was 'in the wings,' waiting on him to finish hammering and sawing, so the rain could begin.

St. Augustine said that patience is the companion of wisdom. So much learning and understanding happens in life's class-room while waiting for Any Day (now) to show up. And while learning and understanding seem good, and even desirable, most of us would be willing to forgo such 'intellectual stimula-tion,' if we could simply get on with our lives. I don't think I know anyone who actually enjoys waiting. In fact, waiting for something to happen any second now or any minute now, or Any Day (now) is so egregious and odious to some of us that we can hardly endure it. Maddening is what it is. Waiting for some-thing to happen, or arrive, or change Any Day (now) drives most people crazy because it demands patience … in the moment.

PERHAPS THE PATIENCE needed for Any Day (now) can best be seen in the ebb and flow of the farmer's life. James, the brother of Jesus mentioned it in the New Testament. In the spring, a farmer plows the ground and plants the seed, knowing that Any Day (now,) the rain will come.

And, before long, the rain does come. The seed germinates. The farmer watches. He waits, once again, for something he expects to happen Any Day (now). Even though his careful examination of the tilled soil every twenty-four hours can't hurry the process along, he still checks his field early each morning. He waits. In patience, he engages in a daily rite of anticipation. Each morning, his examination of the earth demonstrates his faith and belief in a certainty he can hardly wait to see: he knows corn stalks are coming. Not yet, but Any Day (now). And, after the stalks, those tiny ears will form. They always do. They'll grow, just like they always grow. The corn will eventually ripen. Sooner or later, before you can turn around twice — Any Day now — it will be time for harvest.

Like it or not — ready, or not — waiting is a necessary part of life. And waiting can chap a person's hide. Waiting can chafe a person's soul. If something I'm anticipating shows up "on time," it makes the waiting I had to do worthwhile. But, as writer Dorothy Gilman once noted, in her book *A New Kind of Country*, "If something anticipated arrives too late, it finds us numb, wrung out from waiting, ... The best things arrive on time."

She is so right. On time. On time. The best things arrive on time.

However, one of the properties of 'on time' is *specificity*. Three o'clock happens at three o'clock. It doesn't occur at 'about' three, or 'around' three. And the resistance of Any Day (now), or any minute now, or any second now to being tied down to an exact moment frustrates most people. I may intellectually understand that "it" won't be long, now, before something happens. But, waiting around for it to come to pass rarely represents a moment of brilliant living for me. If I stand, patiently waiting for my wife, — who clearly said she would meet me at the Bagel Palace at three o'clock, and now, it's twenty past the hour — when she finally shows up, I don't say, "Oh, I'm so glad you're here, my succulent delight. Now, we can enjoy a majestic interlude of bagels and cream cheese." Instead, I pat my foot and look at my watch. I try hard not to scowl at her. As she shows me a baby dress, or a new pair of 'darling' shoes for one of the grandkids, I don't say what I'm really thinking. I don't say to her, "It's about time." But that's what I'm thinking. It's about time.

If Any Day (now), or any minute now, or any second now is about anything at all, then, it's about ... time.

ONE OF THE clocks on my wife's wall of time is an old school clock. It still works. And when I sit and read in our red chair in the living room, I listen to the tick-tock of that old school clock, and in spite of all I can do, my mind occasionally takes a walk back to my third grade class with Miss Clairborne during arithmetic. We had a clock in that classroom that ticked and tocked me nearly to death during the lifetime they called a year I was in the third grade. I didn't think I would ever get out of the third grade.

(But I did.)

Back in third grade, our classroom clock ticked all day long. We could hear it. We'd have to sit there, working on those dumb old arithmetic problems, and it was so quiet I could hear that clock ticking its cadence, like a woodpecker pecking on a red oak tree, only in slow motion. I could sit there watching the minute hand inch its way around the face of that old clock. But you know what? That clock never displayed the correct time. Not even close. Even though it's hands moved around the numbers, that clock virtually never displayed the correct time. Sometimes, it was three hours fast. Sometimes two hours slow. Although Miss Clairborne made sure that every kid in our class learned how to tell time in third grade, we never depended on that clock to give us the correct time; we never relied on that clock to tell us when we could go out to recess, or wash our hands for lunch, or clean off our desks and prepare to go home in the afternoons.

Instead, Miss Clairborne told us when it was almost time. "Boys and girls," she would say, "The bell for recess is going to ring Any Moment now. Please clear your desks." (Any Moment now is a derivation and abbreviated version of Any Day (now.)) And when our teacher said it was almost time, we knew ... it *was* almost time. However, the fact that we knew recess was close at hand didn't make the waiting any easier. In order to see something hurry up and arrive, I learned that I sometimes have to endure a certain amount of listening to life's metronome tick-off moments.

Miss Clairborne taught me how to *recognize* the times shown on the face of our classroom clock, but it was my wife who really taught me how to 'tell' time. I've already said there's a huge difference between telling time, and recognizing the time, I think.

For example, when I ask my wife what time dinner will be ready, she responds with a definitive answer. Instead of giving me an estimated time, she "defines" the time.

"Dinner will be ready as soon as the potatoes are done," she says. Not a given time that can be found on the face of a clock on her wall of time. But a defined *time*, just the same.

And then I say, "Oh. I see."

But I'm not sure I always do.

EVERYBODY KNOWS they're going to die, but nobody believes it.

Why? Why don't people who know they're going to die believe it until they see it? I think the answer to that question can be discovered inside the uncertainty of another question most of us struggle with: not if I'm going to die, but when? What day? How many days, I wonder, do I have left?

My dad was (as I have come to appreciate in my old age,) at times, profound. "Life is short," said my dad when I was growing up. "One day, you'll turn around twice and notice that your life is behind you." I was cool with that, as long I would be turning around twice 'one day' — a day that's even harder to define than Someday. I believed my dad, I guess. He was right about most things, most of the time. But, learning about the vaporous nature of 'one day on the calendar' wasn't something my dad could teach me, I don't think.

I didn't learn that in school, either. Miss Clairborne may have *told* us everybody dies. But, she didn't *teach* us that everybody dies.

Jacob Few did that.

JACOB LIVED down the street from my brother Dan and me when we were growing up. Jake was a nice kid, and we liked to hang out together and build push carts and play kick-the-can on hot, muggy evenings in Illinois where I grew up. We didn't wear shoes much in the summertime back then. In fact, we didn't wear many clothes at all in the summertime, because it was so hot and uncomfortable. Most of the guys in our neighborhood were as brown as grocery bags (paper, not plastic) by the time summer ended, having spent our daylight hours without a shirt or shoes.

That wouldn't be important, I suppose, except for that fact that when a guy goes without a shirt all summer, there are things you notice about him that you wouldn't otherwise be aware of. For example, I've got a large birthmark on my back, but not many people know it because I cover it up with a shirt, now. But, when I was a kid running around in the hot Illinois summers, all the kids knew about my birthmark.

And everyone knew about Jake's stomach, too.

Jacob wasn't fat. In fact, he was close to being skinny. But he had a big stomach. Bloated, I guess you might say. When we'd stand in front of Mr. Miller's store and drink orange soda out of bottles, the sweat would run down our bellies, carving tiny rivers down the grime on our chests. We'd belch like boys do. We'd chug-a-lug our drinks, like boys do. And, when we were through, we'd hold out our stomachs and see whose was the biggest. We weren't wearing shirts, so we could measure really good. And Jake always won, even though he was the slightest kid on our street. Jacob's gut was always the biggest.

One winter morning, (I remember, clearly: it was "one day") Jake's desk was empty. Jacob hadn't shown up for school. I didn't think anything about it until Miss Clairborne said, with a sadness I'd never before heard in her voice, "Boys and girls, clear your desks, and sit tall. I have something to tell you." Now, it wasn't time for recess. We hadn't even had arithmetic yet. It wasn't time for lunch, either. It wasn't time to go home, or wash our hands, or go to the bathroom. It was time for Miss Clairborne to tell us something we never expected.

Light and quiet filled our classroom that day, as we sat waiting for our teacher to speak. The morning's sun flooded our room. Folded hands. Sitting tall in our seats, we waited. "Tick-tock," said the clock. "Tick-tock. Tick-tock." Waiting. Miss Clairborne sat on her desk in front of us, as if she were waiting for the clock to finish what it had to say.

But, the clock that never told the real time now faded into an unnoticed noise, as with a certain quiet reverence, Miss Clairborne explained how little time any of us really have left.

"I am very sad to tell you that your classmate, Jacob Few ..." And now, her voice broke. And now, tears, which we had never seen from our teacher, began to well in her eyes. She paused for a moment, and then continued.

" Jacob passed away last night in his sleep. He had a tumor in his abdomen which ruptured, and he died suddenly at home." Miss Clairborne continued talking about Jake, his life, and how sad it was, and how she knew we would all be sad, too. But I wasn't listening to her speech very much. In fact, I stopped listening to Miss Clairborne right after her words, '... passed away last night.' Passed away? Who? Jacob? Not Jake? He's only in the third grade. People in the third grade don't pass away? Third-graders don't die, do they? I had never known anyone who had 'passed away.' I remember sitting at my desk, wondering what all of this meant. And I especially remembered thinking that if Jacob was old enough to die ... well then, so was I.

At the end of that day, I had learned something I still remember, and I will probably never forget: One day, I will die, ... and it could be Any Day (now.)

How would my life change, or be different if I 'expected' to die, I wonder? It's a certainty: There's a world of difference between knowing you're going to die — Someday — and knowing you're going to die, Any Day (now.)

The difference between those two days is just a matter of ... time.

3

THE THIRD DAY

E VERY DAY ... For Living

"It is more fun to talk with someone who doesn't use long, difficult words but rather short, easy words like 'What about lunch?'"--Winnie the Pooh

Child, to say the very thing you really mean, the whole of it, nothing more or less or other than what you really mean; that's the whole art and joy of words.

C.S. Lewis wrote, in Till We Have Faces, "

"...life without passion is no life at all. The sober truth is that there is no new life without passion. No baby was ever conceived without passion; no great poem was ever produced without passion; no great piece of music was ever composed without passion. Passion is what takes us beyond the superficiality of life to a deep and wonderful *glow in which we learn to care."* (Elton Trueblood, *The Courage to Care*, from "The Yoke of Christ and Other Sermons.")

I DON'T THINK I've ever told anyone this story. But, it's been long enough now. I guess I can tell you.

One cool March day in the early Spring of 1991, something happened to me that changed my life. It didn't seem like a particularly momentous thing, at the time, really.

My wife and I took a day trip to Sonoma, California. We walked along tree-lined neighborhoods, looking in shop windows and browsing in the quaint little stores. As we sauntered along, enjoying those lazy narrow streets, one particular shop caught my attention.

I would not describe it as a stationery store. That description would not be refined enough for what I experienced when I walked through the door. This store sold fine papers and pens and inks. Oak flooring and wide chair rail around the walls gave the entire shop an air of sophistication. Large bookshelves filled one entire corner of the shop, with dozens of books on how to write, why to write, and where to sell what you write. And, nestled in the midst of those stacks of books, I saw cushy chairs with overstuffed arms, opening to me, and inviting one like me to have a seat. If "the writing life" has a smell, then the aroma of this room intoxicated me, with its hand-made papers, and beautiful pens, and wonderful books about words. I sat myself down. I touched and held and skimmed more than a dozen of those books.

I think, for me, perhaps time "stopped" for a few moments. The literary or musical term for what I experienced could probably be described as a *caesura*, a 'grand pause,' of sorts. A break in the movement. A 'time out.' I must have stayed in that place of words for more than an hour, thinking and looking at books about writing.

I made only one purchase that day in that little shop. I bought something called a writer's notebook. It wasn't anything special, really. Every page contained a quote from some well-known or not-so-well-known writer. Usually, the quotes had something to do with writing, or the creative effort involved in putting pen to paper. But every page also contained empty spaces on which to write notes or jot down ideas.

I left that store having made a decision. In fact, in my memory I can still see myself walking out the door of that little shop, carrying a small brown bag containing that notebook. And on the following morning, March 7, 1991, I sat down in a quiet place with my new notebook. I took out a pencil. (I didn't even use a pen.) I dated the top of the first page, and then I wrote these words:

I bought this notebook for myself. I rarely by (sic) *something strictly for myself, but as soon as I saw this notebook, I knew I wanted it. I have made a decision to become a writer; I will write in this notebook, or one like it, every day.*

But I'm not going to write for anyone but me.

Everyone, I think, needs at least one place in this world where they can be honest — totally honest — without worrying about who may be listening-in. For me, that place will be this notebook. No need for shoes, or socks, or good manners when I write in this notebook. I will think; I will dream; I will act, and move and record with one purpose and end in mind: to gain a better understanding and insight of myself, my God, and my world. I will write my thoughts and tell my stories and describe my scenes for my own growth and benefit. If anyone chooses to come along and watch — if anyone happens by to listen to what I may be saying — if anyone else opens the door to what I think by turning the knob of what I

write, well then, fine. But I choose, from this moment on, to write ...
every day.

I've started nearly Every Day of my life since that March
morning by writing something, either in my journal, or on a
computer. The Apostle Paul referred to the church in Corinth as
a 'living letter, known and read by all men.' I think God wants all
of us to understand that we're being watched; our lives are being
read, whether we're recording what's going on with written
words, or just living life as it comes along.

For me, words matter. Words express who I am, and where
I've been all my life. And I now believe that nothing, apart from
the Bible itself, has shaped me and honed me and affected me
more, both as a writer and as a man, than the discipline of
writing about the story I live and the journey I travel ...
Every Day.

PROBABLY THE SIMPLEST way to define Every Day would be to say
that it's the day 'life' happens. That's why we call it 'everyday
life.' Every Day is the day the sun comes up, and the traffic gets
worse. Every Day, people go to work at jobs they don't particularly enjoy, and come home to houses they haven't paid for yet.
Every Day is the day the six o'clock evening news comes on at
precisely six o'clock. People go about their lives, picking up the
laundry at the cleaners, or dropping the kids off at school.
Babies are born and old people die and I get one day older,
Every Day. Every Day, rituals and traditions are formed. Life
Every Day can look a lot like life every other day.

Sometimes, we even attach the names we've assigned to the
days of the week to Every Day. We can get paid Every Friday, for
example. In other words, every week, Every Day happens every

single day, and sometimes, it's even a weekly event. For example, Every Sunday, some people sit in the same seat at church. They hear the same preacher. But, they don't leave church the same way they came in; whether they acknowledge it or not, they are changed. Every Day, in fact, they change. Certainly, Every Sunday they change. For, to be in the presence of God is to be changed. (Ask Moses, if you don't believe me. All Israel could tell he'd seen God, after he came down from that mountain conversation, just by the way his face looked.)

In many ways, I think Every Day moves slower than the rest of the days move along. Perhaps that's because of what happens Every Day. Our character, for example, is formed because Every Day we practice our belief systems until they ultimately become 'ways of life.' The habits we get into, the paths that are worn in the grass on college campuses, the calluses that appear on a carpenter's hands, all those things occur because God gave us life ... Every Day.

Waves come ashore Every Day, too. Relentlessly, and in a cadence measured by God himself, waves of life wash ashore. Unannounced, yet fully anticipated and expected. Some huge. Some barely a ripple on the surface. Wave after wave, day after day, Every (single) Day. Whether I'm at some beach house to hear the noise and feel the spray or not, I know the waves are at the shoreline. They always are. There's no stopping those waves. Who would want to?

And, there's certainly no stopping the waves of monotony and repetition that find their way into my life Every Day, either. Whether I know what's happening or not, whether I'm watching, and listening, and paying attention, or not, wave after wave of unrelenting 'life' will come ashore all around me Every Day. Maybe that's why Every Day is so tricky. Every Day can sneak up on a soul, if he's not careful.

I WATCH PEOPLE EVERY DAY. I notice them. And certain people seem to possess a rhythm that drums along, and a beat that accompanies their march through life. They walk an ordinary walk, casting an ordinary shadow. Life seems plain, and not dressed up, for so many people these days. When 'those' people wear their Every Day clothes, they look different than when they dress up. It's hard to make Every Day 'special,' in that sense. Life Every Day can lull a body to sleep, like the sound of the ocean's waves.

But the fact that Every Day is so ordinary doesn't mean that it isn't complex. There's nothing 'simple' about the way Every Day life plays itself out. Even though Every Day is exactly the same length of time as every other day, each has a cadence and meter all its own. The wrinkles and twists and turns of life make Every Day as unpredictable as the weather. When I flip my desk calendar to a new day each morning, Every Day life shows up on that new page, ready or not. And navigating the daily perturbations of that life can be a real challenge.

Like all the other days God has given us to live, Every Day is incredibly important. What we do Every Day has profound implications in determining where we ultimately end up. Character is formed a day at a time. Habits are cultivated a day at a time. If we want to keep our weight under control, we would be wise to watch what we eat Every Day. If I want to be physically fit, I may not have to work out Every Day, but I will need to develop a lifestyle of maintaining fitness. And developing that kind of lifestyle will need my attention ... Every Day.

So how *do* I manage Every Day? How do I keep Every Day in proper perspective? How do I enjoy the unique freshness of Every Day, while managing the routine, and ebb and flow of normal life?

For me, it's a matter of recognition, and definition, and spelling. I have to make sure I don't confuse Every Day with something that sounds suspiciously similar: everyday.

MARK TWAIN SAID that the difference between the right word and the almost right word is the difference between lightning and a lightning bug. I believe that's true. There are times as I pour over a sentence like the one you're reading right now, that I have to pause and ask myself: *Oops! Is that right? Is it "as I pour over" or is it "as I pore over?"* I stop. I think. I examine, and re-examine, and check to make sure. And if I did use the wrong word (which in this case I intentionally did) then I correct myself. I change, " ... pour over" to "pore over." Both words are *good* words, but both words are not the *right* word. Both words *sound* the same. But that's where writing gets tricky.

And that's where life gets tricky, too. Sometimes, the way life *sounds* is so wonderful. But the way life is lived is so ... well, so not-so-wonderful.

Just as there's a huge difference between a good word and the right word in writing, there's a huge difference between "the good life" and "the right life" in living. Granted, when it comes to living our lives, the distinction can sometimes be confusing, but the litmus test seems simple enough: The way to tell whether you are living an everyday life or Life, Every Day is the same way you tell the difference between a lightning bug ... and lightning.

Trust me, you know it when you see it. You know it when you feel it, too. The difference is unmistakable.

Saying the very thing you really mean to say with your life — nothing more or less or other than what you really mean to express with your life — is not that easy. Most people, I suppose, know the difference between 'everyday' and Every Day. *Everyday* is an adjective. An 'everyday' something has no remarkable feature to set it apart.

My wife has everyday dishes that we eat on unless we're having company. (If we have company, I have to get the good dishes down from the cabinet. Don't ask me why the only time we eat on the good dishes is when company comes. That's just the way life is.) Our everyday dishes are fine for us to eat on, most days. And, we eat everyday food on those everyday dishes, too. Meat. Potatoes. Frozen corn. *Everyday* is routine, and habitual, and common as a pot roast. (I heard some guy on the radio the other day who said the only difference between a rut and a grave is the depth. He's right.) Most of us use the word *everyday* nearly Every Day, to describe what's normal, or regular, or the usual. In fact, some people think Every Day is a synonym for 'boring'.

But I'm convinced that God never intended Every Day to be as *everyday* as a stalk of celery or a bowl of vanilla ice cream. The beautiful ninetieth Psalm is a written conversation which the inscription says is, 'A prayer of Moses, the man of God.' And as Moses, the man of God wrote his prayer, I believe he began to think about Every Day. He asked God to teach him something very important. He said, "Teach us to number our days, that we may gain a heart of wisdom." (Ps. 90:12, NIV) Moses knew how important God intended Every Day to be; that there was a world of difference between saying, *everyday life happens,* and, Every Day, LIFE happens. Whereas *everyday* runs together, with no space for punctuation, or some grand pause, or reflection, Every Day is unique, and one-of-a-kind, and possesses a date all its own, a number among all other numbered days.

One of the reasons I think Moses thought it would take God Almighty Himself to help us with keeping track of the number of our days is because most of us don't use numbers, when it comes to counting on life happening, Every Day. Instead, most of us use what I call the "living by rote" method (which, by the way, is not even remotely close to the idea of living by faith. But that's for another day.) Some people make life Every Day so boring that it has transformed itself into something even God would never have dreamed of. Life Every Day has morphed into a flavorless existence, bland as tofu, and boring as a television commercial you've already seen ten thousand times. Everyday *life?* I call it *everyday limp.*

I know some people — not you, and not me, but some people — who get up in the morning, and they brush their teeth and then they take a shower, instead of *ever* doing it the other way around. They mindlessly pour (or is it *pore?*) themselves a bowl of corn flakes each morning; cornflakes with bananas on them, no less. They read the *daily* paper ('daily' is another word for everyday, you know.) In fact, some people actually read the obituaries — Every Day — as part of their daily routine. Is that boring, or what? As their everyday life unfolds, they commute to work; they drive the exact same route five days a week, no detours, no deviations.

I'm not unsympathetic to people who struggle to depart from their normal routine, mind you. I'm no different than anyone else. In fact, unless I pay close attention, I'm as vulnerable to life in the mundane lane as the next guy. Invariably, when ordinary things dictate and dominate the ebb and flow of my life, I can easily begin to believe that Every Day is a yawn, and filled with meaningless minutia.

I may even miss the bigger picture.

In his "Letters to Malcolm," C.S. Lewis wrote:

"I sometimes pray not for self-knowledge in general, but for just so much self-knowledge at the moment as I can bear and use at the moment; the little daily dose ... You and I wouldn't, at all stages, think it wise to tell a student (speaking as a teacher) exactly what we thought of his quality of work. It is much more important that he should know what to do next ... The unfinished picture would so like to jump off the easel and have a look at itself."

That last phrase has been rattling around in my head like a loose screw in the bottom of a bucket: "... The unfinished picture would so like to jump off the easel and have a look at itself." What is it, do you suppose, about unfinished pictures, that compels us to want to look at them?

Last year, my wife and I went to San Juan Capistrano in Southern California to see if the swallows would show up again. Such a lovely place, really. Quaint shops, and of course, the mission, which is quite impressive. While we were there visiting, I noticed several people with easels and paints. Sitting for hours, staring, and then touching brush to paint, and paint to canvass, they worked in silence. In fact, they almost assuredly worked this way, Every Day.

I was drawn to their work, (pardon the pun.) I had an irresistible urge to stand behind them and watch them work. And I was joined in my peeking by several other people; people I didn't even know. An odd mix, really. Total strangers, standing behind total strangers, watching art 'happen.' What is it, do you suppose, about human beings? Most of us have an insatiable urge to peek over a painter's shoulder to see what the picture looks like, even though it isn't finished yet.

I'd like to think my curiosity isn't really nosey-ness. But I'm not so sure. At the very least, my need has its roots in something *inspective*, I guess you could say. I have a need to inspect the artist's work. How much does what he's painting look like the real deal? How good is the painter at capturing the scene he's trying to paint?

Or maybe, I peek because I'm curious about the artist's *perspective*. What does he see that I'm missing? Or maybe I'm curious about how the painter creates emotion, and shadow, and feeling on a flat canvass by using mere paint? I'm not sure, exactly, why I have a need to peek over the shoulder of the painter. I only know ... I do.

I don't know how many painters I've watched in my lifetime. The wharf in San Francisco is home for several sidewalk artists. I love to watch them create with chalk. I've watched artists working on oil paintings of Half Dome, in the Yosemite National Park. I remember peeking over the shoulder of an old woman sitting on the rim of The Grand Canyon, who worked in her sketch book, with charcoal. I even watched a guy with water colors sit and paint a field of wildflowers in Austria near the spot where Julie Andrews sang, "The hills are alive with the sound of music." (Quite honestly, his 'hills' didn't look as alive as the ones in the movie.)

Sometimes, the unfinished work I've peeked at over the years has been pretty good. Other times, it wasn't so good. In fact, (now that I think back on it,) there have been a few times, when the work-in-progress I was looking at wasn't as good as I thought I could have done myself. (I saw a guy trying to paint the Old Red Mill in Alley Springs, Missouri once. Granted, he wasn't finished with the painting when I saw it, but his mill looked more like a maroon or reddish-brown shoe box turned up on edge than it did that Old Red Mill.)

In all my years of peeking, however, — in all my experiences

at looking over the shoulders of various artists at work — never
once have I given suggestions on how things could be, or should
be ... *different.* I've never patted a guy on the shoulder who was
working on a painting and said, "You know, I think the sky
you've painted needs a few flying birds." Or, "Have you given any
thought to putting more leaves on that tree?" I've never
mentioned to some sidewalk artist in San Francisco that she
needed to work on the eyes of the face she's trying to draw
because they just don't look right to me.

That's not to say, however, that I've never given my opinion
on a work in progress. How about you?

I've looked over the work of The Master many, many times.
In fact, I'm not above 'peeking' at what He's up to Every Day. I
have an entire lifetime of memories. Times when I couldn't wait
to see how the picture would turn out. Times when I wanted to
peek, even though I couldn't. Times when I was anxious. Times
when I didn't like the way things were shaping up.

I have definite ideas about how I think life is suppose to look.
When the picture I see is different from the one I expect, you
might say I become somewhat of an 'art' critic. Funny how I'd
never do that with a sidewalk artist drawing in chalk on the
streets of San Francisco, but I don't have any problem at all
giving my opinion to God — The Creator Of Heaven And Earth
— about how my life Every Day is shaping up.

And I give that opinion... before He's even had a chance to
finish the bigger picture He's working on.

I wonder why that is?

∾

I'M CERTAINLY NOT unsympathetic to artists who have to discipline themselves to focus on their work. I've already mentioned
the decision I made back in 1991 to write, Every Day. That may

sound great on the surface, but having spent the last many years now trying to be faithful to what I said I would do, I've come to understand the daily challenge my commitment represents. Like most people I know, I'm pretty busy. In fact, it's not uncommon to hear any of us refer to how busy we all are in our everyday lives. But when I get busy with everyday life, how in the world do I manage to sort through and write about life Every Day?

I mean, think about it for a minute. Try to put yourself in my shoes. When I sit down to write, sometimes I get confused. Well, actually I'm not so much confused, as I'm "confronted." I'm confronted with a significant dilemma: where to start? What should I write about? Every Day, I have to decide what to write about everyday life. And that's not always so easy.

To prove my point, let's pretend. Let's pretend I'm sitting down at my computer, and I'm going to write something, Today. I'll let you follow my thought process. Maybe it will help you understand my predicament ... a challenging predicament I face Every Day of my life.

Picture me, now. I'm sitting at my computer. Since, quite honestly, as I look around, I don't see much going on, Today, I think I'll write about my everyday life that happened *Yesterday*, instead. (I hope that's okay.) But that presents another dilemma, now that I think about it. When I write about Yesterday, what should I include, I wonder, and what should I leave out? I mean, a lot of 'everyday life' happened Yesterday that I could mention.

I could write about making that pot of coffee I brewed Yesterday, I guess. I'm always the first one up, usually around five or five-thirty. Within a few minutes of my feet hitting the floor, I started the coffee. I remember it perfectly. I grabbed our bright red coffee grinder from under the cabinet. Opened the freezer and grabbed the coffee beans. (Someone said to put coffee beans in the freezer. It doesn't make sense to me, but that's where we keep them, in the freezer door, right next to the frozen corn.) I ground the coffee beans. I measured the ground coffee. Four scoops. (My wife says I make coffee too strong). I filled the coffee maker with cold (not warm) water, and turned that baby on. I put the grinder away under the cabinet. I put the coffee beans back in the freezer door. And, I waited. I didn't wait for the entire pot to drip through, though. I never wait. As soon as there was enough coffee for one cup, I poured myself some.

Now that I get to thinking about it, making coffee doesn't sound that interesting. Maybe I should write about how I fixed that drawer for my wife, Yesterday. We have such a beautiful dresser in our bedroom. But the outer loveliness of our dresser belies the inefficiency of the glides on the undersides of the drawers. In other words, the drawers don't work. The glides evidently weren't glued properly at the factory, and Yesterday, my wife asked me to repair and re-glue one of them. I needed some of that "super-bondo" type glue. I have two tubes of it ... somewhere. (We keep our coffee in the freezer, but we're still working on a specific place to keep the super-bondo type glue.) Before I could fix the drawer, I had to find the glue. Actually, Nathan, my son, found it for me. He said he found it in the cabinet above the washing machine, next to where we keep the spare light bulbs. (I've got to remember that.)

I repaired the drawer. Quick job, really. But, as they say, 'before the super-bondo glue could dry,' my wife had another project: a shelf in our bedroom in desperate need of hanging (or is it "desperate need of being hung?" No matter.) I measured. I leveled. And, then I took my drill and screwed two screws into the wall. Both screws —yes, I said both of them —twisted off and I had to find two more screws. More measuring. More leveling, before I finally got the shelf hung.

Yesterday had so many 'everyday life' happenings in it, I hardly know what to include, really. I could tell you about my cutting the grass on our riding mower, and how I drove under that apple tree we have on the south side of our house. The apple tree that's in full bloom. The one that has low-hanging limbs. I drove under one of those limbs while I was cutting the grass yesterday, caught my shirt on a snag and tore it nearly off my stupid self before I could get the mower stopped. I think that's pretty interesting.

Or maybe I could mention that my wife didn't cook dinner last night. Instead, we had take-out Chinese. I had Mongolian beef; she had sweet-and-sour-something. Dinner last night was very interesting.

I need to keep these chapters short, though, so I guess I won't be able to tell you about a lot of other things that happened Yesterday. I won't have time to tell you about my friend's trip to the doctor, and the fact that his cancer is back. Did I tell you he called? They told him his pain would be severe but they said they can keep him comfortable with medication. The doctor said he's never had a patient like my friend, who says he settled dying with the Lord several months ago. If I had more time, though, I'd tell you about it.

I don't have space to mention my friend from Mexico who came by Yesterday, either. He lives across the field from us. Barely making it, financially. Trying to feed a family of six or seven, I don't know. Sometimes, I think I can see the sadness in his eyes when we visit. He said he needs sixty hours of work a week in order to have enough to barely make it. He wanted to know if I had any little jobs he could do around the house here. (Too bad I'd already fixed the drawer and hung the shelf, huh?) I gave him some money, but it wasn't enough, I know. I'd love to spend more time telling you about our conversation Yesterday, but I guess it will have to wait.

If I had more time and space, I could tell you about the homeless guy with the dog, too. I passed him on my way into town yesterday. A man with long hair and a dirty beard, carrying a little old spotted dog, walking along on the side of the road. (Did I mention it rained yesterday?) Anyway, I've seen both of them around before. One of these days, I need to stop and talk to that guy, and ask him about that dog. Ask him, 'What's up with that?' What's his story, I wonder? Too bad yesterday was already so full.

If I had more space, I suppose I could mention the call I got from my youngest son, Yesterday afternoon. He works nights at a hospital, and mentioned a kid he tried to help; a thirteen-year-old with swastikas carved in his arms. My son wanted to know my opinion on how he could help the kid. I told him I'd have to think about it and get back to him. Maybe I'll call Tomorrow. Maybe.

Oh, and on the way home from the bank Yesterday? I stopped at one of those little coffee huts to order a cup of coffee at the drive-up window. When I pulled up, the girl said they had to brew some more coffee, and I'd have to wait for four or five minutes. "Would that be okay?" she asked. Can you imagine? Can you imagine waiting four or five minutes for a cup of coffee at a drive-thru coffee hut window? I mean, I do that in the morning, when I make my own coffee, but at a coffee hut? That's ridiculous! I was ticked. I told her I was ticked. I asked her how a place that's suppose to sell coffee ... can run out of coffee? And then I said, no, that I *didn't* have time to wait four or five minutes, and it wouldn't be okay. I asked her if they still had *cappuccinos* for sale, and could I get one of *those* in less than four or five minutes.

I didn't tell her I was a writer, though, or that I wrote witty, inspirational essays. I didn't mention that I was a committed follower of the teachings of Jesus Christ, either. It didn't seem relevant. And, anyway, I didn't have time. As I drove out of the place, I remembered again how rushed I was, and how terribly busy everyday life had already become. I didn't have time to wait on coffee. It's all I can do to try to make sure I'll have space in my days for important and weighty things; things I can actually write about, things I should actually *care* about Every Day.

Now, maybe you can see what I mean about *everyday life* having an impact on my creativity. If I had never decided to keep a journal, I'd have it so easy. I'd never have to figure out what to write down and what to leave out of my story. I wouldn't have to pay so much attention to what's happening all around me, like I do, as a writer. Since I don't paint, I don't have to be troubled by how many birds are in my sky, or whether to add more leaves or take some out of my work in progress.

Or do I?

The more I think about it, the more I wonder if, maybe I'm not paying enough attention to what to leave in and what I take out of my everyday *living*, I don't know. Are writers and painters the only ones who have to deal with the fact that in the midst of living our everyday lives, we need to take care not to be oblivious to things we see Every Day? I wonder? If I don't keep a journal, if I never sit on some beach to paint the waves that come ashore Every Day — if I don't sit down in some over-stuffed leather chair and enjoy a pause, so the smell and atmosphere of the creative process at work within me can permeate my life Every Day — I may not even be aware that I'm being watched; that there is an Audience of One, who keeps watch, Every Day; the One who never needs to peek over my shoulder to see how the work-in-progress called *me* is coming along.

He already knows.

4

THE FOURTH DAY

Y ESTERDAY ... For Remembering

'Do not say, "Why were the old days better than these?"
For it is not wise to ask such questions.' (Ecc. 7:10, NIV)

"When I was younger I could remember anything, whether it
happened or not."
(Mark Twain)

Several years ago, I saw a cartoon in a New Yorker magazine that cracked me up. Two polar bears were having a conversation, one of them sitting on an iceberg, and the other in the water, looking up at his friend. The bear on the iceberg says, "You know, I've thought a lot about it ... and I am really cold."

I don't know what it was about that cartoon that caused me to howl, but it struck me as really funny. And, this morning, I had a sort of 'parallel' thought. You see, in a couple of months, I hope to have another birthday, never mind the number. And, like the polar bear on the iceberg, I've thought a lot about it.

And I am really *old*.

I READ IT AGAIN, a few days ago in The Book. One of the writers of Psalms wrote,

> "For all our days pass away under your wrath, our years come to an end like a sigh. The days of our life are seventy years, or perhaps eighty, if we are strong;"

— Ps. 90:9, RSV

All my life (and especially during my twenties and thirties) I thought that anyone who made it into their sixties was *really* old. Now, I'm thinking, "Bummer. Where on earth did the time go?"

I already know that some people who read these words — people who are older than sixty or even seventy, for sure — will say, "You aren't old; you're just getting started.' I don't believe it for a moment. (No runner who's running a race would even begin to start it, if they were as out-of-breath as I am!) Sure, some people are still kicking around well into their eighties and nineties. My dad, for example, lived in his own home, back in Illinois until he died at eighty-nine! I know that some people age well. I'm just not sure I'm one of them. I suspect that some of my weariness — some of the 'oldness' I feel— stems from the truth of a quote I read in "Gilead,' the wonderful novel by Marilynne Robinson. One of her characters quipped toward the end of his life, "It's hard to understand another time."

I agree.

I live in "another time," and different from the one that used to be. Today, things are nothing like they were, just Yesterday. Church is different, now. And society is certainly different. Music and art and entertainment and so many other things in our culture are drastically different from any other time in history. (I just filled my gas can for my riding lawn mower. It cost me sixteen dollars for five gallons of gas. (It seems like only Yesterday that I could buy gas for two dollars a gallon, or was it twenty-five cents a gallon?)

Yes, I've thought a lot about it. I am *really* old.

It's true. When I was younger, gas didn't cost so much. And music in church actually had a tune; (that's not a complaint, just an observation). I'm sure things were slower, when I was younger. I'm in the first class of baby boomers, and we played outside during the summer time when we were kids. We watched black and white television, and went to drive-in hamburger stands.

Growing up was even more dramatic for my folks. They walked three miles to school in the snow, and their shoes had holes in them. (I've often wondered why they didn't build the schools a little closer to where people actually lived?) They didn't eat store-bought groceries; they had to grow their own food. Can you imagine? They had to eat green beans from a garden? And, they didn't have black and white television when my dad was a kid. People had to sit around in the evenings and actually talk to one another, or listen to the radio for entertainment. Some people even (God forbid) read *books*. Can you imagine?

I've outlived my culture, perhaps. Or, maybe it's just hard to understand another time. What will my kids and my grandkids have to brag about, or complain about, or survive, or endure? Will they say things like, "When I was a kid, we had a dial-up modem to get on the internet?" What sorts of things will my kids remember as 'markers' for their culture? I wouldn't know where to even begin guessing. That's probably because I hardly know where to begin trying to understand the culture that now surrounds my life.

YESTERDAY IS the longest day you will ever live, and it's getting longer all the time. No matter who you are, no matter the number of days the expanse of your life will ultimately contain, Yesterday *happened.*

Of all the days God has given us, Yesterday is the only one that grows with each passing moment in time. You may not have given it any thought lately, but on the day each of us was born, our Yesterday began. Before that — before the day we were born — there was no '*us*', and there was no "Yesterday" *for* us. Yesterday is where we've been all our lives. Every breath we've ever taken. Every idea we've ever conceived. Our tears. Our joys. Our successes, and our failures. The record and recollection of all our moments prior to this very moment in time — all of these are held in the repository of Yesterday. And, it is the connection of all of those moments and events that represents the plot and course and *story* of our journey: the life God has allowed us to live.

Yesterday is the only day that grows longer with the passing of time. It's the day preachers talk about most when they offi- ciate at the memorial services of people who have died. When pastors reflect on those lives, their focus invariably revolves around memories and accomplishments, words spoken, acts of kindness rendered, events that happened ... Yesterday. Often, family members bring pictures of the deceased to memorial services; awards and plaques and memorabilia and "remember- ings." But, what those loving family members are really doing is organizing and presenting life's journal entries and recollections of their loved one, things written down and duly noted in the documentation of life lived Yesterday.

Yesterday is an easy day to recognize, really. As our lives move along that road and race that has been marked out for us, in the rearview mirror of our journey, God has given us the ability to see a reflection of what we've been up to all our lives. Without Yesterday, there would be no day for us to look back upon. And if we couldn't look back, an important part of our understanding and appreciation for life would go wanting. As we live the moments of our lives, our Yesterday lengthens; our memories deepen and expand. And the experiences we have lived through, somehow, change us at a very deep and visceral and "profoundational" level. The wrinkles in my brow, the decreasing number of hairs on my head, the halting gait in my step, all of these represent the reality of time marching on, in spite of all I can do.

And all of us are in the same parade of days. The older we get, the more Yesterday is filled with the remembrance of the minutia and mania of the journey. An interesting fact, I think: Researchers have discovered that infants smile as many as 900 times a day, while those of us who have lived to be sixty-years and older smile, on average, three times a day. I wonder? What happened along the way to living 'life' that caused the frequency of smiles to change, do you suppose?

Perhaps, we don't give enough thought to the hilarity and sobriety of the happenings contained within the day we call ... Yesterday.

~

You take, for example, our living room couch.

Memory is a funny thing, isn't it? I don't mean *funny,* as in 'Ha, Ha'. But it's funny what you can remember if you put your mind to it. Some things are just *naturally* easy to remember. A first car. A first date. A wedding day, or the birth of a child. Those kinds of things seem to find a permanent place in our memory, I suppose for obvious reasons.

But, sometimes things pop into our memories that we haven't thought of in a long, long time; things nondescript and hardly worth remembering. For example, the other day, I sat eating a bologna and cheese sandwich. I hadn't had a bologna sandwich since I was just a kid.

Somehow, as I sat there eating my sandwich and staring off into the distance, a picture of the *décor* in the living room of the house where I grew up on Myrtle Avenue in Granite City, Illinois came into my head, clear as the bottled water I was drinking. I didn't have to stir up my memory. I didn't have to work at it. I just *remembered* our living room and the way it was decorated. It's a little difficult to adequately describe our living room in the house where I was raised, but I'll try.

No one ever told me (nor did I ever ask) what the "color scheme" in our living room was suppose to be. The tile on the floor was a shade of brown or beige, about the color of a burlap bag, with little specks of God-only-knows-what-color blotches sprinkled across each individual tile. I think my dad got that floor tile "free" — or at least really cheap — when he remodeled our house.

Now, *ugly* is a good word to describe ducklings that "don't look too good". But *ugly* is a beautiful word compared to a description of that brownish, beige-ish colored tile in the living room of the house where I grew up. I think one of the reasons that the tile seemed so bad was because of the couch we had in our living room.

I've been in some family rooms and some living rooms that have beautiful couches with wonderful fabric on them. My brother, Dan, used to have a great couch in his living room. Big flowers all over it. When my wife and I would go visit his family, I'd take naps on his couch because it was so comfortable. My Aunt Laine and Uncle Bill had two or three nice couches in their house, too. Everybody in my extended family could show up after church on the same day, and not one person would have to stand up because they didn't have a place to sit. The reason? My aunt and uncle had three or four really nice couches.

But when I was growing up, we didn't have a nice couch in our house. That's not to say we didn't have *any* couch. We had a small couch in our living room. But it didn't smell too good. Well, I think that's an understatement, really. Our couch stunk. I don't mean metaphorically. I mean, literally our couch stunk.

But it didn't always smell bad. I guess you could say the bad smell just sort of 'showed up.'

One evening, as we all sat watching television — probably "Gunsmoke" or some such program — my dad announced that he thought he saw a tiny little field mouse running across the floor during one of the commercials. My sister put her feet up on the couch, at that point. (We didn't usually get to put our feet on the furniture, but I guess my dad gave her a special dispensation of grace, because she was afraid of mice.) Anyway, he told my mom we needed to set a mousetrap just to make sure we didn't have a "mouse problem."

But, my mom was a humane sort of woman, God rest her soul. And she chaffed at the idea of the violence of a mousetrap.

"I am *not* handling a mousetrap with a dead mouse in it," is what she actually said.

Instead, she had a better idea, a better "mousetrap" for that mouse. She bought some mouse bait. (In a word, *poison* was what it was.) With great tenderness, she set that box of poison out the next day. That stuff must have been guaranteed, because it sure-as-the-world worked. Within a week or so, my momma got her field mouse.

Have you ever heard the expression, "I smell a rat?" Well, I know where it came from, because after that tiny mouse got a belly full of that poison, he must have crawled up into our gray couch, found himself a secluded and totally hidden spot, and died like the rat he was. We turned that gray couch upside down and right side up for weeks looking for that dead field mouse. We never did find him, but we knew he was there. Believe me, we knew he was there. Consequently, I never did take a nap on our couch after that. (It wasn't that good for naps, anyway.)

Our couch was gray. Battleship gray. (Please refer to an earlier paragraph of this story, in which I mention that the tile in the living room was brown.) At the risk of using poor grammar to make an emphatic point, let me just say at this juncture, "GRAY DON'T GO GOOD WITH BROWN."

My wife taught me that one morning as I was getting ready for church. I had on my brown, pinstriped suit, and a brand new pair of gray socks, and she said, "Take off those socks. They don't go with that brown suit."

I said to her, "Yeah, gray goes good with brown because we had a gray couch and brown tile in our living room when I was growing up." And then she said, "I can't help your tile, and I can't help the couch and I certainly can't help the way you "grew up." I *can* help *you*. Change your socks. They don't go with that brown suit." My balloon popped. My wife forever altered my idea of what goes good with a brown, pinstriped suit.

But I digress. The couch.

It wasn't just the *color* of the couch that was problematic. Our couch had a character and 'gripping' personality all its own. The picture of that couch sticks in my mind to this day. Maybe it sticks in my mind because of the way it stuck on my body.

The couch was not only gray. It was naughahide. Now I'm not exactly sure what a "Naugh-ah" looks like, but it's hide can make you sweat when you try to lie down on it. And in the summer time, when I was already hot and sticky, if I'd sit down on that couch and its 'gripping' personality, my skin would vulcanize to its surface in spite of all I could do. If company came to visit, and I was sitting on that couch, and my dad or mom said, "Scoot over and let your uncle Bill sit down," I couldn't scoot.

Stuck like lint on a sucker.

Maybe that's why I thought of that old couch the other day while I ate my bologna and cheese sandwich. No wonder there are times when I feel like I'm stuck? I've got all kinds of memories of things crammed into the storage spaces of my life; stuff I never have been able to reconcile; things that didn't seem to go together; events and people that just didn't match up. I've had a lot of rotten things sneak around the corners of my life, too. How about you? Some of those things weren't that big on the surface, I guess. But the sticky truth is that almost anything that crawls into the crevices of a life can bring death and dying with it, if it finds a place to sit and fester. Even though I occasionally catch myself declaring my own innocence, as I hide behind my carefully couched words, somewhere beneath that gray deceit, even the smallest things can be odious to the soul if you don't deal with them right away. Poisoned memories. Stuff you end up never, ever forgetting. Stuff you remember, whether you put your mind to it or not. Stuff you remember whether it even *happened* or not. Stuff that amounts to nothing more than a bunch of bologna. Stuff that came to pass ...Yesterday.

INTERNALLY, most of us live our lives as islands unto ourselves, I think. The Wise Man wrote, 'Each heart knows its own bitterness, and no one else can share its joy." (Prov. 14:10, NIV) I think there are times when most of us struggle with wondering how we've done managing our lives compared to everybody else. And "running" our lives the way most of us do can resemble a bewildering and confusing journey, similar in some ways to that character in Frederick Buechner's story in *Secrets in the Dark*, whom he described as "lost in the forest somewhere, the unenchanted forest of a million trees."

The litmus test for determining what we believe about the quality and value of our lives has its roots in what we believe, and how we evaluate our Yesterday.

Madeline L'Engle was right when she said,

> "I am still every age that I have been. Because I was once a child, I am always a child. Because I was once a searching adolescent, given to moods and ecstasies, these are still part of me, and always will be ... This does not mean that I ought to be trapped or enclosed in any of these ages ... the delayed adolescent, the childish adult, but that they are in me to be drawn on; to forget is a form of suicide ... Far too many people misunderstand what 'putting aways childish things' means, and think that forgetting what it is like to think and feel and touch and smell and taste and see and hear like a three-year old or a thirteen-year-old or a twenty-three-year-old means being grownup."
>
> — MADELINE L'ENGLE, A CIRCLE OF QUIET

Big difference, it seems to me, between growing older, and being 'grownup.'

I am convinced that every living soul leads a storied life; a life which contains a plot, a drama, a reason for being. And, each life's storyline can best be read and understood by a careful examination of the past. Each person's journey is, of course, different from all others. Yet, all human souls share one common denominator: a life-path that is replete with celebrations and sorrows, bends in the road, woundings and wonderings and scars that mark the way we have travelled.

All kinds of 'stuff' clutters the landscape of Yesterday. Shame, and guilt can hide there. So can regret. And all our warm and fond memories live there, too. Some of what we remember is wonderful; some of what we remember is so bleak we wish we could erase it, like chalk letters written on a blackboard. How many times, I wonder, have I *thought* those words: 'What was I *thinking*? How could I have been so stupid?' How many times have I said — either to myself, or aloud so anyone standing nearby could hear — "If I had that to do over, I'd do it differently," or "Thank God I don't have to do *that* again!" or, "I'd sure love to do *that* again." Every time I make such a statement, I'm expressing either my gratitude or my chagrin about an encounter or an experience that occurred ... Yesterday.

Each moment and defining experience in my life has its own unique meaning, like the words in some sentence, or paragraph or story. (That must be why some people say they've lived a *storied* life?) Each moment I live becomes part of a bigger picture that grows and expands, becoming more complex with the passing of time, like some giant snowball rolling downhill, that grows as it rolls along the ground. There's a certain 'once-and-for-all' aspect to all our life experiences. No moment in Yesterday is like any other moment in time. Each moment is totally unique. There is no such thing as a 'do-over' in life. Like the manna of old, life's experiences have a way of evaporating before our eyes, as each day's sun makes its way across the horizon of our lives.

But the fact that there are no "do over"s doesn't mean there aren't a lot of "do again"s. Life's experiences have a way of repeating themselves, have you noticed? The fact that I went through a challenging experience once, is no guarantee I won't ever have to go through another challenging experience as long as I live. And the fact that I've had a particular *kind* of test or trial once doesn't mean I won't have that particular kind of challenge again. (If I've had one difficult person to deal with in my life, I've had a hundred! And yet, they were all different.)

And, certainly, the fact that I accomplished something once does not guarantee that I will be successful at it the next time I try, either. Each success is different from all the others. And each sorrow and challenge is different from all other sorrows and challenges. That truth helps me see and appreciate the complexities and incredible potential for learning made available to me through the 'looking glass' of Yesterday.

If I pay attention, if I 'go to school,' — if I sit up and take note, and stay awake in life's classroom and carefully examine where I've been — I can benefit from a degree of wisdom and knowledge that grows with the passing of time. I will learn in ways no book could ever teach me; my memories represent an 'institution of higher learning.' I gain an education I earned the hard way, in the laboratory of life's many and storied experiences.

And the name of that 'institution of higher learning?'

The School of Hard Knocks: A school that was founded and established ... Yesterday.

WHEN I WAS ten years old, I invented the cell phone.

Well, technically, I guess you might not say I 'invented' it. In fact, it might be a stretch to even say I thought of it, (now that I'm thinking about it.) It wasn't exactly a cell phone that I invented. What it was, was a device my brother, Dan, and I could converse on without actually seeing each other, which is sort of like a cell phone, only different. And, as is often the case when people dare to take a stab at new and untried things, the experience was, shall we say, 'painful.'

Richard Jansen lived across the street from us. He and I were the same age. We had the same teacher. We went to the same school. He mentioned one fine spring day that he'd heard somewhere — or maybe he read it in a Boy Scout manual — that a person *might* be able to actually make a kind of "telephone" if they had some string and two frozen orange juice cans. I listened carefully as he described what sounded to me like a really good idea. I didn't act too excited, though, because I didn't want Richard to think my brother Dan and I would steal his great idea, and an invention that could be such an incredible boon to society.

So, we waited. We waited until Richard finally went home. (His sister, Cloe came to tell him that his mom said, "Come home to eat. Supper is ready.") And as the sound of the door closing behind Richard could be heard in the front of our house, the sound of Dan going through our garbage could be heard in the backyard.

Like men on a mission, we scoured our garbage for orange juice cans. We didn't drink a lot of frozen orange juice at our house when I was a kid. And we didn't have a single can in all our garbage. But, the Dublins lived next door. They were old people, very nice. My brother suggested, "Hey, Mr. and Mrs. Dublin are pretty healthy. Maybe they drink frozen orange juice?" We both bolted to their garbage can, and (no kidding, this is really the truth) we found not one, but two frozen orange juice cans with one of the ends missing. Perfect. We were almost there!

The parts list for this invention couldn't possibly have been simpler. In addition to the two frozen orange juice cans, we'd need a long piece of good, stout string. In the ends of each of the cans, we'd need to punch a pair of holes, small ones, but big enough for the string to be looped around and tied. We raced to my dad's toolbox for some really strong string. My dad was a carpenter. Fortunately for Dan and me, he had an entire roll of really cool line. We could have stretched that string all the way across the street to the Jansen's house, if we hadn't been concerned that Richard would look out the window while he was eating and see us putting our phone together. We couldn't risk discovery, though, so we cut the string long enough to be fun, but short enough to be clandestine.

If we had written an operating manual for our device, it would have been pretty simple. One short paragraph: After tying the ends of the string to the cans, stretch the string tight. One person (that would be me, since I invented it) would talk into the open end of one of the cans, while another person (that would be my brother, Dan, who was eighteen months younger than me, and needed lots of practice "listening" anyway) would hold the other can up to his ear, and listen.

Only four things now stood between us and our first conversation on our phone. We needed four holes, two in each of our confiscated cans, so we could thread the string through and tie it. The ice pick. All we needed was the ice pick to punch our holes.

My mom was a very organized person, and she kept the ice pick in that drawer next to our kitchen sink, just to the right of the knives and forks, and just to the left of her grocery sale coupons. I knew exactly where that ice pick was. What I didn't know was what my momma would think of me 'playing' with her ice pick.

When Dan and I walked into the kitchen and started

rummaging around in what we called the 'knife and fork drawer,' she objected. (Note: There were also spoons in the knife and
fork drawer, but since Dan and I often had to wash the dishes,
we had very little use for the spoons in the knife and fork
drawer. But that's a different story.)

"Are you being careful in that drawer?" asked my spitfire
mom. "There's nothing in there for you. Are you messing up my
grocery sale coupons?"

"No, momma. I'm being careful," said I. But those words had
no effect on my momma. (No matter how well-chosen my words,
they often had no effect on my momma. She was not a "word"
person. She was more like an 'I-am-woman-hear-me-roar'
person.)

As the words, "I'm being careful," came out of my mouth, the
ice pick I had grabbed was coming out of the knife and fork
drawer. And, when my mother saw the ice pick, she changed her
sentence structures from *interrogatives* to *declaratives*. She
stopped asking questions, and started giving instructions. (Actually, they were more like 'laws' than instructions.)

"Oh no you don't. Put that ice pick back. You'll hurt yourself."
A point she intended to make. My mother was obviously picky
about who used her ice pick. I had no idea.

"We're making a string phone," I said. "We need holes in
these cans."

"Not now," she said. "Maybe after supper, your dad will
help you."

Now, Dan and I had cut thirty or forty feet off a brand new
string line we found in my dad's toolbox. (Oh. Did I forget to
mention that the string line was new? No matter.) It was not
difficult to imagine that my dad would not be happy seeing his
new line stretched between two frozen orange juice cans, with
me on one end and Dan on the other. I thought it unwise to
overtax him with unnecessary requests. Dan and I would wait

for the coast to be clear before proceeding with our phone assembly plans.

After supper that evening, I noticed my mom and dad looking for car keys, and my mom gathering her coupons from the knife and fork drawer. "You guys do the dishes while we're gone," she said. "Your dad and I are going to the grocery store. We'll be back in an hour or so."

"But," I said, "what about our holes? Can you do those before you leave?" That seemed like such a reasonable request, really. But my mom replied, dispassionately and seemingly without reason, "Not now. Maybe when we get home. But leave that ice pick alone. You'll hurt yourself if you try to use it."

As two parents drove away from their house on Myrtle Avenue to go to the grocery store, the oldest of their sons went to school. Not a "regular" school. Not the school and classroom he attended with Richard Jensen, Monday through Friday every week. No. The school he went to that warm, spring evening was for an education that was a *special* education school. An 'obedience' school. Or perhaps, it could better be defined as a 'disobedience' school.

Class time started as the car drove out of sight. First, the squeak of a knife and fork drawer opening. Then, an ice pick being removed. An orange juice can, touched, and steadied by a guilty left hand. The raising of a right arm; the falling of the same. And then, the sound of weeping and gnashing of teeth that often accompanies rebellion and disobedience. Impaled by impatience. A suffering wound, endured in silence. (To have told my mother when she returned would have been 'mother-assisted-suicide.')

Even though long-since healed and nearly invisible in the webby flesh between my left forefinger and thumb, my sorry hide now hides an exquisite scar, an ice-pick-shaped wound. Once open and bleeding, but now healed and barely noticeable;

irrefutable evidence that I have traveled, and survived, and learned and been touched by something that happened ... just Yesterday.

ONE OF THE ways God has chosen for reminding us of the journey we have travelled is by giving us the gift of 'scars.' Each and every external scar on my body represents a kind of mile-marker in my life: evidence of an occasion when a 'wounding' occurred, whether I expected it or not. On my physical body, I have dings and dents in my carcass that represent an encounter with a nail I didn't see, or a window I broke with my head. In addition to that, as Yesterday gets longer, what I like to call "age-appropriate wrinkles" just begin to show up in the mirror, whether I expect them to or not. Those wrinkles scar and mar my otherwise stunning visage. (What's up with that?) I even have scars that surgeons intentionally carved into my skin with exquisite precision and care, as they 'fixed what was broken' inside of me.

It's not fashionable in today's culture to celebrate the scars we carry around with us. I mean, when's the last time you went to a plastic surgeon and asked him if he would give you a visible scar you could enjoy looking at? No. No, we don't *celebrate* our scars. Most of the time, we want to *camouflage* those scars, keep them covered up and out of sight.

But the physical scars that mark my body aren't the only scars I possess. There are other kinds of scars, you know? Those *internal* scars I carry around Every Day serve as a testimony to a different kind of wounding: a life-wounding that occurred Yesterday. Those etchings in my soul represent a roadmap of the detours I've taken, and the life-scars I've acquired while I've been having the time of my life.

Those unexpected "stabbings-in-the-back" by people I thought I could trust, or worse yet, those self-inflicted "shootings-in-the-foot" that I somehow manage to survive — all of them represent challenges I've had to overcome, or survive, or persevere. Internal scars represent character-marks that forever change the visage of my inner man; blemishes and imperfections in my soul that make my story one-of-a-kind, like a fingerprint, and unique to me alone.

It's important, however, to understand that there's a big difference between a scar and wound. A wound gapes open, painful and bleeding and depleting me of my life and energy ... now. Wounds are *now*. Wounds live in the present. Scars, on the other hand, are about the woundings I have survived.

With time and God's healing grace, a scar can replace the pain that was once a wound. I'm very grateful for the scars in my life, because they give me confidence that healing can happen, that healing *has* happened, that I can survive the woundings of Today. I can go on living; I can 'live' to fight another day's battles.

And the surviving of the wounds produces character in my life.

IN MANY WAYS, I think our scars can represent 'trophies,' then; trophies of survival that certainly deserve a place of honor in our lives. We place them on some imaginary mantle, representing God's sustaining grace and love.

There can be all kinds of trophies on that mantle. Some of them have come at great personal sacrifice and effort. Some of those trophies represent the accomplishments and achievements of my life. What about the books I've written, or the awards I've won, or the mountains I've climbed? What about the career I've had, or the family I'm so proud of? A life well-lived, after all, does have its rewards. The joy and recognition of a life lived in excellence is a very real thing, and rehearsing and recalling the achievements in our lives, our careers, can be such a nostalgic, if not altogether accurate, activity. (One old man I know put it this way: 'The older I get, the better I used to be.')

We often derive warmth and comfort from the pictures we paint in our minds of those happenings chronicled in Yesterday's moments. Perhaps that's why Annie Dillard wrote in her book, *The Writing Life*, that she loved to write in a room with no view, so "imagination can meet memory in the dark. " It is true: The older we get, the more precious Yesterday's recollections can become.

One of the challenges of successfully addressing Yesterday is balancing the memories of our storied lives. How shall I celebrate the victory and 'romance' of my journey, while not becoming overwhelmed by my ineptness and failures and woundings along the way? Successfully navigating life "in the moment" must involve, then, not becoming too fixated on where we've been all our lives. There will be a day for a final remembering; a memorial service to remember where we've been all our lives.

But not Today.

Perhaps that's one of the reasons the Apostle Paul, in The Book, said he was forgetting those things which are behind, pressing toward the mark. And Isaiah, the old prophet recorded a good word in the Good Book about Yesterday, too. He wrote down what God had to say about where the nation of Israel had been all their lives. He said,

"This is what the LORD says — he who made a way through the sea, a path through the mighty waters, who drew out the chariots and horses, the army and reinforcements together, and they lay there, never to rise again, extinguished, snuffed out like a wick: Forget the former things; do not dwell on the past. See, I am doing a new thing! Now it springs up. Do you not perceive it?"

Isa. 43:16-19 (NIV)

I can appreciate and savor the unique mix of scars and sorrows blended with the gratification of my accomplishments and the achievements of Yesterday. To dwell in Yesterday's memories for too long isn't profitable for me. And yet, I've discovered that many of the solutions I need for Today come out of what transpired in my Yesterday. I guess you could call it 'experience,' or perhaps, wisdom. Yesterday contains the pain I'd rather forget strangely packaged up with the joy I love to remember.

I heard a guy on the radio Yesterday. He was some kind of a sports psychologist, I think. Sorry I don't remember his name. It's been too long ago. But I do remember something he said. He said he thought that all awards and trophies that athletes receive should be presented in the form of bananas. "Everyone knows," he said, "what a banana looks like after it's been sitting on a mantle for a few weeks."

He wasn't saying trophies are bad. They're just not 'lasting.' Times change. Circumstances change. Life marches on. And along the mile-markers of that march, I would do well to celebrate my battle scars and successes by imagining them to be bananas on my mantle. I'm so grateful for all the trophies I can point to, as testimonials to what I have survived or been able to accomplish with God's help.

But His mercies, says the old Song Writer, are 'new every morning.' While I would do well to glance at where I've been, my more important task is to keep my eye on where my life is Today, and where I might plan on going. One thing is certain: Yesterday's room called 'remember' contains experiences that have a limited "shelf-life." And as I hold a loose grip on my Yesterday's successes and failures and woundings and sorrows, I guard against the danger of living in the past. "Do not say," said the Wise Man in The Book, "Why were the old days better than these? For it is not wise to ask such questions." (Ecc. 7:10, NIV)

We all do it, I suppose. Looking back can be such a rewarding exercise. It's easy to see how faithful God has been. And if I'm not careful, it can be easier, still, to lament the 'if-only' wishes or the 'what-might-have-been' scenarios in my life, doing irreparable harm to this very moment in time, this "Today" I have to live.

Because of that ever-present danger — the danger of living a life of regret about what might have been — one final thought, then, about Yesterday: It comes from a Chinese Proverb, which says, "The best time to plant a tree is twenty-years ago; the next-best time is ... Today."

All I have to remember *now* is, 'Where did I leave my shovel?'

5

THE FIFTH DAY

T ODAY ... For Now.

> *"He made the moon to mark the seasons,*
> *and the sun knows when to go down."*
> (Ps. 104:19, NIV)

> *"But encourage one another day after day,*
> *as long as it it still called Today, ..."*
> (Heb. 3:13 NAS)

> *"Give us today our daily bread."*
> (Matt. 6:11, NIV)

> *"Today is your day! Your mountain is waiting.*
> *So. . . get on your way."*
> (Dr. Seuss)

Going to school for the very first time can be a scary thing. Learning is often that way. Scary, I mean. It's been awhile now, since I was in the first grade. Yet, I still remember my mom walking with me to school, and how I felt, leaving her safety and entering a world of learning, and challenge, and 'getting along.'

When I walked into my classroom in first grade, on that very first day of school, my teacher, Miss Kenny (yes, that was her real, last name) seemed likable enough. She smiled. She pointed to my seat, which she had already assigned to me before I even arrived. She knew exactly where I was to sit. Over by the windows; the windows that had big, apple-green letters taped to them that could be read from the street, "Welcome to School!" I didn't know anyone else in my class. I sat down in my chair, wondering what it would be like to go to school Every Day.

And I wondered what I would learn.

But, anyone who's ever been to school before knows that on that very first day, students don't do a lot of school work. That doesn't mean they don't *learn*. It just means there's not a lot of actual school work on that first day. All kinds of other educationally important things happen on the first day of school.

Students receive their books. They go over the classroom rules. (Miss Kenny had a lot of rules. Stuff like "No chewing gum," and "Always raise your hand until you are called upon to speak," and "Keep your hands to yourself," although some of the kids had already violated that rule before she could mention that it was against the rules. Who knew?)

That first day, we spent a lot of time 'getting acquainted, I guess you could say. We played some cool games at recess. Miss Kenny assigned us to what she called "learning circles," even though some of us had no idea what we were suppose to actually 'learn' in our circles. It was a pleasant day at school for me, that very first day. I remember it well. Part of the reason I can remember it so well is because of the *project* Miss Kenny assigned the last hour of the day.

She walked down each row of our desks, carrying a stack of

paper plates. Each plate had a name printed on the back of it, and as she walked down each aisle, she delivered the plate to its owner. Every kid in our class had their very own paper plate. Then, she instructed us to leave our desks, and find a seat at what she called "art tables" at the rear of the class. It was a little congested for all of us to move at once, but obediently, we all found a seat around the art tables.

"Each of you have your own plate," she said. "Before we go home today, we're going to make something beautiful for our mothers, to show them what we did today at school." On the tables in front of us were bowls filled with colored beads, and small scissors with rounded blades so we wouldn't poke ourselves or our neighbors. ("No poking" was already a class-room rule, but she must have felt a need to repeat herself.) Miss Kenny had provided cotton balls, colored kite string, tape, and two or three bowls of that white paste-glue, too.

Our room seemed quiet as a library. Miss Kenny walked from seat to seat, continuing her instruction, and already peering over our shoulders. Quiet. Miss Kenny definitely wanted *quiet* in the room.

We sat obediently waiting, every set of eyes glued to our teacher. "First, take the hand you do NOT write with, or throw a ball with, and place it in the middle of your plate. Spread your fingers out wide. Then, take a pencil or pen in your other hand, and draw an outline of your hand on your plate, like this." She turned to the chalkboard behind her, and with a piece of yellow chalk, she outlined her own hand, her fingers spread.

"When you've completed that task, look up at me," she said. "No talking." (I decided, in first grade, teachers must need to say that a lot.)

Seconds ticked by, as the sound of thinking, and the 'look' of concentration filled the room. Careful tracing. Tongues out. Attention to the detail of drawing the outlines of our first grade hands onto paper plates. When every set of eyes had looked up at Miss Kenny, she issued her final instruction.

"Now, choose some of the materials that are on your tables, and glue them onto the edges of your paper plate. Make a beautiful design. And, when you go home, you can take your lovely art work home with you, so your parents can see what you made for them today at school."

I've never been too 'arts-ee' but that first day of school, I threw myself into my task with reckless abandon. I had carefully traced my hand's outline on my plate. Now, I planned. I thought. I chose my beads and cotton and string with great consideration. I glued. (I have to be honest. I also peeked at the plate of the girl sitting across from me. I don't remember her name, but she had a great idea of winding some of the string around the tracing of her handprint. It looked so good on her plate, I decided to add that idea to my plate, too.) I concentrated. I focused. I created what I thought was the most beautiful paper plate I had ever seen, a plate with globs of glue, and carefully cut strips of colored paper, and kite string, and cotton balls smashed all over it, with an outline of my hand smack in the middle. It was, in a word, *magnificent*!

When school ended that day — when the bell finally rang — I could hardly wait to see my mom, and bring her what I had made, what I had created just for her. When I handed her my beautiful design, she hugged me.

"For me?" she asked, in a way that told me she already knew the answer. And I said, "Yeah, momma. It's for you. I made it." She told me it was just what she wanted, that it was beautiful, and she was so proud of me. She noticed my printed name on the back of the plate, and that seemed to be very important to her, for some reason. My name, on the back of the plate, and the beautiful art work on the front.

I remember her asking me one question about my very first

day at school. She said, "Did you learn a lot of interesting things Today?"

And I said to my mother, "Yes, momma. Today, I learned where I'm suppose to sit, and I learned some rules, and I learned how to put my handprint on a paper plate."

And my mother said, "Wonderful. Amazing."

And when we arrived home, she posted my artwork ... on our refrigerator door.

THIS WILL BE the shortest chapter in this book, because it's about Today. And, no matter what else happens in my life Today, this will be the shortest day I will ever live. The length of Yesterday grows with each passing moment in time. And, for certain, the *certainty* of the day called Tomorrow may never materialize. But Today? No matter what else happens, Today will be twenty-four hours long, whether I live through it or not. If life represents a test, — if I survive the challenges of Today — I already know that I will not have crammed more learning and living into this day than exactly twenty-four-hours can contain. When midnight comes, I'll have to start cramming for the test all over again, whether I even *want* to or not.

Today is 'right now.' Today is the present day. It contains and includes the breaths I now take, the beats of my heart at this very moment in time, and the blinks of my eyes. Today is the only day that literally 'is.' Today is the day I'm typing these words into my computer. And Today is also the day you're reading my words. Different dates on the calendar. But the exact same day for both of us: Today.

Today is a 'touching' day, I guess you could say; the day I get to embrace things, and people, and ... life. I get to do something about Today. It's the 'for sure' day, and a gift from God. If I make a move, if I make a decision, — if I make a difference, — well then, Today will be the day it will have to happen.

If Today could be located on one of those maps they have at rest stops along the Interstate, Today would be marked with a big arrow that says, "You are Here!" Today stands all by itself on the calendar of my life. It is totally unique to this very moment, and different from all others I have ever, or will ever, live. When the poet, Horace, wrote "*Carpe diem ...*", the 'diem' he meant to be 'carpe'd — the day he meant to be seized, or 'plucked' was ... Today.

Today is 'unavoidable,' you might say. No dodging. No ducking. No escaping a pivotal truth: No matter how I feel, no matter where I am, or who I *think* I am, Today is right in front of my nose. Today is an in-your-face-day. It will not be ignored. It cannot be postponed. It's here. It's *now*. If I'm anywhere at all, at any given moment in time, well then, it must be Today. Today's the day people ask questions about. "What's your schedule, Today?" or "What time will you be home, Today?" or "What's the weather forecast for Today?"

Those kinds of questions underscore the fact that, in one sense, Today is a 'predictable' day. And yet, in another sense, Today is totally unpredictable. The weather Today can be like a bitter north wind that blows on a winter's night. Or it can be like a warm spring breeze that makes me want to fly a kite or click up my heals. Somehow, Today just *feels* different than any of the other days.

Successfully navigating Today takes a particular focus and belief system, I think. I would almost call it a *theology*. Almost. But not quite. It's a belief system that has its roots and foundations in what may seem to be a very strange place: a refrigerator door.

I will tell you what I mean.

HAVE you noticed how much you can tell about a person, or a family by what's on their refrigerator door? Over the last several years, I've made a habit of carefully observing the refrigerator doors of the homes of people we go to visit. All kinds of homes. Doctors' homes. Friends' homes. The homes of folks in our church. And all their refrigerator doors are different, with stuff displayed that is unique to their own families. Even our relatives have things on their refrigerator doors I would never have imagined.

Some folks tape calendars to their refrigerator doors. Last week, I saw a school lunch menu posted on the side of a refrigerator door for the coming week. (Today, they're serving chili.) Dentist appointments. Scripture verses. Pictures of family members, grandkids, post cards from people on vacation in Mexico. Grocery lists. Store coupons. Amazing stuff stuck on the doors of refrigerators.

There's an entire industry out there, totally dedicated to helping people festoon their refrigerator doors. Where do people find those magnets? The ones shaped like ice cream cones, and Mount Rushmore, or the Sears Tower in Chicago, or chocolate cupcakes? Magnets with little clippies on them. Magnets with pithy sayings written on them. (We have one on our refrigerator door that says, "Nothing tastes as good as thin feels." But I don't let it keep me from opening the freezer door for an ice cream bar.) You can tell so much about a family or a person by just observing their refrigerator door.

But what connection is there between a belief system and what's on a refrigerator door?

I HAVE NOTICED in my life a certain 'ebb and flow' of energy that occasionally plagues me. By profession, (and I believe, life-calling,) I'm a writer, a pastor and an executive and physician life coach. Much of my day can be filled with writing about people, listening to people, coaching people. But, the 'draw-down' factor in my life can be significant. Like some flashlight that's been left on all night, my batteries weaken over time, I think, and the potential light in my life dims unless I 'recharge.'

A couple of years ago, I was feeling particularly depleted and drained. To be honest, I was having real doubts about whether my life was really 'measuring up' in many areas. A friend told me of a retreat center which was part of a Benedictine Christian community located on the East Coast. He thought it would be a perfect spot for me to spend a few days rejuvenating. At the encouragement of my wife, I made plans to spend a weekend on Cape Cod, attending a retreat for souls like me who needed refreshing.

On that first Friday evening, I sat in a circle with fifteen other men: a Catholic priest, an engineer, an insurance executive, a marketing guru. Men from all walks of life. Men very different from me. And yet, men exactly like me; men needing some restorative encounter that would refresh their lives and inner souls. During that first Friday evening meeting, we were asked what we were anticipating. What did we hope would occur during our weekend stay? One-by-one, these total strangers shared a bit of their stories, and expressed their desire for what the next few hours might hold for each of them.

But, when my turn came, I found myself unable to really articulate what I wanted, what I might need, what I really expected. I finally said, "I guess I'm here to 'hear.' I'm going to try to listen to my life, and perhaps determine what I might need. I'm not sure what I expect." All of the men in the circle seemed accepting of my non-answer, and as I walked to my lovely room after the session, I truly questioned why I'd even come.

Saturday morning, after a great breakfast, we all sat around a large table, waiting for instructions on the activities of the day. The leaders of the spiritual retreat walked into the room, carrying a small basket to the front. One of them explained that in the basket were slips of paper with scriptures on them; bible verses had been selected by some of the members of the community there. The leaders said that a group of folks in that community had already been praying for those of us who would be participating in the retreat. They had selected and typed several different verses on the slips of paper. And, in the selecting, they had prayed over every single piece of paper, every verse, asking God to speak specifically to each individual recipient in some eternal way. The leader of the session walked to the end of the table, and handed the basket to the insurance agent, who sat in the first chair.

"Please take a slip of paper, and pass the basket to the next person. Do not read what's on your slip until directed to do so." Quietly, almost reverently and one-by-one, each man chose a slip from the basket as it made its way around the table.

Perhaps it was the quiet of that moment that gave me pause to think. I don't know. I watched that basket make its way around the circle, as it passed from one man's hand to the next. I studied each man, watching his face as he took a random slip of paper out of the basket like some school boy, following directions on the first day of school. I noticed a kind of solemnity or ritual that I felt was taking place, here.

And yet, in all honesty, I also wondered if this didn't feel a Christian version of a fortune cookie without the cookie. I wasn't exactly cynical; perhaps *skeptical* would be a better word to describe my initial thoughts, as that basket made its way around the circle toward me.

And then, a conversation took place.

It was not an 'out loud' conversation. It was an 'inside voice' conversation. As I watched that basket slowly being passed, a question entered my sorry mind. I do not know whether it was God's voice posing the question, or me, talking to myself. (My inside voice is at times virtually indistinguishable from God's, you know.) I heard a question being asked: "Do you believe you were led here ... to hear?" And of course, regardless of who was asking that question, I had already determined that I had come to hear something about my life. *Yes.* The answer to that question was an undeniable, 'Yes.'

But then, quickly following on the heals of the first question's answer was another question: "Do you believe God can speak to you in this way?" Again, I do not know who asked that question of my inner man, but I do know what the correct answer was: "Yes. I believe."

The basket continued to slowly pass from one hand to another. And as my hand reached into the basket for my own specific piece of paper, my heart slowly changed from one state to another. Inside, in my inner man, where no one else could see, that small piece of paper became very dear to me, even though I had no idea what words were written on it. I had come to hear from God, and learn from Him. If He chose to speak to me through a tiny slip of paper, I was open to what He might be saying.

Our instructor told us that after we chose our piece of paper, we would be given an hour to meditate on what it said to us, and then, we were to create some work of art to describe what we had experienced. It could be a poem, a story, a picture, a sculpture out of clay, or any other artistic expression we chose. They had gathered materials, paint, clay, glue, and equipped a large room with tables and chairs in which to finish our assignment after we had spent time in meditation.

"You are now free to go. Walk these grounds. Find a quiet place to think. Find some listening post. Sit and listen. We believe God will speak to you about what he would like you to know. And, after you have listened, and after you sense that you have heard from Him, create some expression of that experience to share later in our sessions this evening. You may now read your verse. And then, you may go."

Like little boys anxious to open Christmas gifts, each man unfolded his slip of paper, reading what it said. And then, like monks on their way to morning prayer, each man rose from the table in absolute silence. One by one, each man left the room. Everyone ... except me.

For many moments, I sat at the table, alone. I could not move. I did not *want* to move. Over and over, my eyes rehearsed the words written on my tiny slip of paper. Words that snuck up on me. Words I had not anticipated. Even though I had read this verse in the Bible, perhaps hundreds of times before, I knew as I sat there at that table that I had never really *heard* those words in just this way before. My weary and dry and questioning self began to be 'watered' by that Living and Sapient Word, as it seeped into the very core of my inner man.

And this is what was written on *my* slip of paper:

> *"Behold, my servant whom I have chosen,*
> *my beloved with whom my soul is well-pleased."*
> Matt. 12:18-21

I knew, of course, the moment I began to read, that these were words written about the Lord Jesus. The Obedient Servant. The Humble Carpenter. God Become Man. This was a verse about Him, not me. A beautiful description of The Savior. I've taught on the verses of Matthew's gospel many times. But, as my eyes began to read these familiar words, God somehow let me see my own human and worthless self in the midst of them. All the other men had quietly left the table, already planning, perhaps, what they would paint, or draw or sculpt. But me? I simply sat for many moments in that quiet place, reading those words — the wonderful things God had said about his Son, ... and the wonderful things I was now convinced He believed about me, His son.

Servant.

Chosen.

Beloved.

With whom my soul is well-pleased.

Never had I ever imagined such lofty words could describe me. How could I have missed it, before? Over and over, I read. In this quiet place, and deeply moved, I read and re-read those words; words I thought I knew so well, and yet, words I had never known in just this way before.

For I was now convinced that as my God looked at my feeble life, He saw the very life of Jesus in me.

I finally left that dining room, and walked the short distance from our retreat center to the ocean, and lovely Cape Cod. I sat on a bench, looking out across the sea, imagining. And yet, I could not imagine. How could God look into the empty vault and inadequate recesses of my life and be 'well-pleased?' What of my failures? What of the ineptness of my feeble attempts at serving? So many of my efforts were childish and immature. I had so much to learn about true servanthood. And even the 'successes' I might have pointed to in my life, when compared with the 'all-surpassing power of His greatness,' they seemed so puny and paltry, not even worth mentioning. How could God be 'well pleased' with one like me? What did these words *really* mean?

And then that scene came back to my remembrance. (Was it God? Was it He who reminded me? I do not know.)

I could, with perfect clarity, see that desk and chair over by the windows in Miss Kenny's first grade class. The letters taped to those windows, and the green letters that spelled out, 'Welcome to School.' I remembered the classroom rules, too. Rules I violated before class had even had a chance to begin.

And the learning circles. Those circles of learning and teaching I would be a part of. And the table in the back of the room. The table, covered with colored beads, and worthless strips of construction paper, and cotton balls, and scissors and paste. I could envision myself sitting that day in first grade, turning my plate over so I could see my name printed on the back of it. A mark of ownership. A mark of identity. This was *my* plate, and no one else's. It might look like someone else's plate; it might have similar components. But my plate was different than any other, and as I sat there gazing out over the Atlantic and Cape Cod, I could see myself working on that paper plate and its design. I remembered the tracing of my small and immature hand. Worthless beads and strips of paper, glued with such child-like precision, and creating a collage of indiscriminate pattern and form.

Finally, after many moments, I remembered *her*. My momma, who was my greatest encourager. The one who birthed me, and loved me unconditionally. The one who took me to school, and had faith in me the entire time I was there. My mom, who seemed so delighted with my 'beautiful' gift for her. And when I handed it to her, she hugged me, and she thanked me, and she told me how beautiful was my lovely art, and how it was just what she wanted. With total clarity, I remembered that I never once heard her mention that my gift to her was just common, ordinary kite string and cotton balls and colored beads glued to a paper plate.

And she displayed my worthless art ... on our refrigerator door, so that anyone entering might notice what an incredible son she had, with such incredible gifts, and producing such amazing and beautiful art.

After many minutes sitting at the ocean that day, reflecting on my slip of paper with the scripture written on it, I left my listening bench and walked to the art room, a grown man feeling like a little boy about to create an art project on the first day of school. Along the way, I picked several wild flowers and dried grasses that grow in such abundance along the shores of Cape Cod. When I entered the room, I sat down and took a large piece of paper.

Carefully, then, and oh so carefully, I traced an outline of my own hand. And I glued the wild flowers and dried grasses onto that page. Simple. Plain. Using ordinary and yet incredibly intricate and beautiful things God himself had created, I tried once again to take an empty space and glue something remarkable to it in a way that would bring joy to the heart of One I love.

When I was finished with my simple creation, I took it back to my listening post. And I held it up to Him, the Creator Of All There Is, the Giver of Every Good and Perfect Gift. Like some innocent first-grade school boy, I found myself, once again, presenting my art work. My name on the paper. My handprint —the handprint God Himself had etched in my palm — on the page. And common flowers glued into place; flowers God himself had made. All of this I held up to Him. I heard myself weeping softly, and saying, "Here, Father. I did this *Today* during my time of learning."

As I sat there, alone except for Him, I didn't hear God mention that the flowers and grasses I used were ones He had already created. He didn't call attention to the fact that they wouldn't last, and that before the sun would set, Today, my creative genius would be dry and colorless.

Instead, I truly believe God called all heaven into rapt attention as I sat there with Him. In my inner man, that place where

God uses his 'inside voice,' I heard Him call heaven to order: "Have you seen this? Have you seen what my beloved child has brought to me? Have you noticed the devotion and care with which he fashioned something he thought I would love? And it has his handprint — the handprint I gave him — all over it."

In my mind's eye, I could see Him as He took my innocent depiction of devotion to Him... and He placed it on some great refrigerator door so that anyone entering the halls of heaven could see. And He smiled, and He carried-on, and He hugged me, and loved me, and He pointed to me ... and said, "Behold, my servant whom I have chosen, my beloved with whom my soul is well-pleased."

IF TODAY IS ANYTHING, it is a 'touching' day; a day for touching ... and being touched.

You may not have given any thought to it until just this very moment in time. But this morning, when you got out of bed, you began to *touch* things. The night stand. The door knob to your bedroom. The lock on the bathroom door. When you reached for your toothbrush, you left a faint trace that you had touched it, that it was Today, and time to start actually living, again. You began to indelibly mark the objects you touched, and you left evidence that you had passed this way. The fork you held at breakfast. The door of the car, as you opened it to drive to work. Today, you've already touched hundreds, or maybe even thousands of objects, leaving your fingerprints. All day long Today, you've left evidence of where you've been

Of course, that's not a revelation. Everyone knows that as we 'go through' life Every Day, we leave behind our fingerprints and our DNA as an unseen testimony to the fact that there was a day when we lived this life, and walked this way. Most of us don't *intentionally* leave fingerprints on the things we touch. I guess you could say, "Fingerprints just happen."

But what if fingerprints didn't just '*happen?*'

How would Today be different if I made a *conscious* decision to *intentionally* leave my fingerprints all over the world I encounter Today? What if, when I got up this morning, I decided to leave as many fingerprints on my world as I could possible manage? What if I decided to touch as many people Today as I possibly could?

Fingerprints may be invisible to the naked eye, but that is not to say they are insignificant. In so many ways, and at so many points along my journey, Today, I've had opportunity to touch someone around me. A smile. A wave. A word of encouragement or help. *Small* things are not the same as *insignificant* things.

Think about where you've been Today. Who have you seen? Who have you talked to? How did God change, encourage, or help them along just by the sheer fact that they encountered you? And how have *you* been changed, encouraged, helped along your journey, just by the fact that you encountered them? When your feet hit the floor this morning, what did you 'intend' for Today? How *intentional* have you been Today at leaving traces of the imprint of Jesus, and your faith and life journey on those who are around you?

For a certainty, you've left a mark. While it may seem insignificant to *you*, I promise you, it isn't insignificant to God. He's already designed your every act of kindness, every expression of His grace, every effort of love, no matter how insignificant it may seem. God has no need for the 'art work' of my life or yours. He can speak and a universe is formed. No, God has no *need* for our puny efforts. But He brings glory to Himself, and takes incredible delight in my presenting Today and all it holds, up to Him. As I acknowledge the truth that my efforts are by His grace alone, and represent an expression of my dedication and commitment to Him, *He* receives the honor.

I believe that one of the tragic mistakes I can make in my life Today is taking myself, and my paltry efforts too seriously. God's not fortunate that I'm on His team. But, perhaps an equally serious 'under-sight' might be my not appreciating my life in Him and His powerful enabling for impact *seriously enough*.

Today ... my life matters to the people I decide to touch, because God made me to be a 'toucher' of those I encounter Today.

My life matters to God, too. He's intensely interested in what I'm up to, Today, as I manage life's classroom and all the stuff I think might be on my plate.

He created me.

He created every good thing that's on my plate.

And Today, when He looks at me, He sees "Servant, chosen, beloved, with whom my soul is well pleased."

6

THE SIXTH DAY

T OMORROW ... For Sure?

"Free Crab Tomorrow."
    (Sign on the side of Joe's Crab Shack in San Francisco)

"... you do not even know what will happen tomorrow."

— James 4:14, (NIV)

I HAD the opportunity to speak to a group of doctors at a medical school and hospital in New York City awhile back. The doctors who had come weren't wearing their 'doctor faces,' really. They weren't wearing their white coats — those starched jackets they often wear that have their names embroidered over the lapel pockets. Instead, they wore casual clothes. They were 'off-duty,' relaxed, and as they entered the meeting room, I enjoyed hearing them laugh and visit. (I don't think doctors laugh enough, when they get together, but I digress.)

Almost-larger-than-life-paintings of impressive-looking men hung on the walls of the oak-paneled conference room where we had gathered. The doctors in those paintings all wore academic gowns, some of them with funny-looking hats on their heads, and large, important-looking medals around their necks; medals that obviously represented awards they had received, honors that had been bestowed, or Nobel Prizes they had won.

It's always a little bit intimidating for me to talk to doctors. As I stood before that group, and the paintings on the walls, a certain poignancy seemed to present itself. I changed what I had planned to say, and instead presented those gathered with a word picture.

I asked the doctors to imagine with me that I was handing an empty, brown paper bag to the doctor in the first seat of the front row. "Imagine," I said, "that I've asked this doctor to place everything he knows in this bag; everything he knows about medicine, everything he knows about fixing a car, all he knows about the English language, or growing tomatoes, or the German Requiem, by Johannes Brahms. I want him to put all he knows about EVERYTHING in this bag."

Some of the doctors smiled. Some of them looked rather quizzical, as they wondered where I might be going with my word picture.

"After this doctor has placed all he knows about anything and everything in the bag, he will pass the bag to the next doctor, who will then place all *he* knows in the bag. We'll continue passing the bag around the room until everyone here has had a chance to put the totality of all they know into the bag. And then, let's imagine that we can also pass the bag to the men in these impressive paintings hanging on these walls, asking *them* to put all *they* know into the bag, so that by the time we're done with this bag, we will have the collective 'knowing' of every person represented in this room."

And I twisted the top of my imaginary bag, and pretended to carefully set it on a nearby table, the way I would if I didn't want any of the information it contained to spill out.

"Now," I said, "we'll take another bag and do the same sort of exercise. But this time, we'll put everything we DON'T know in this other bag." And I held up another invisible bag.

A sort of collective smile began to drift across the faces in that conference room, as doctors — doctors who all *know* so much — began to think about putting what they *didn't* know in a paper bag. One of them, a doctor in the back of the room, spoke up and broke the silence with a declaration:

"We're gonna need a bigger bag."

And so it is with Tomorrow. If we were each to place what we *don't* know about Tomorrow in a paper bag?

We'd need a very large bag, indeed.

I TOYED with the idea of leaving Tomorrow out of this book, because Tomorrow can easily be confused with (and is somewhat similar to) Someday, or Any Day. Like those two days, Tomorrow isn't here, yet. But there are also some other discernible differences between Someday, Any Day, and Tomorrow.

Someday, as we've already seen, is a lot further away from *now* than Tomorrow. No need to get too excited about Someday. It'll come along in it's own sweet time. If I'm actually going to get *excited* about a day, I am most prone to get excited about Any Day (now), because Any Day (now) may arrive any minute now, and will almost certainly be here before I know it.

It's the 'before I know it' that complicates Tomorrow. I try to *know* Tomorrow before it gets here. I try to know the weather Tomorrow, so I can plan my picnic. I try to know which horse will win the Kentucky Derby Tomorrow, so I can place my bet, Today. I live my life as if the *coming* of Tomorrow is a sure thing, a sure bet, and since I act as if I *know* there will be a Tomorrow, I'd also like to know what it will contain before I have to live it.

The 'sure thing' about Tomorrow, however, is its lack of surety; Tomorrow is not for sure.

Tomorrow is the only day in our lives that 'shrinks' with the passing of time. As I'm in the process of living my life Every Day, my Yesterday — and the road I have travelled since the beginning of my life — grows longer and longer, while the path containing all my Tomorrows grows shorter and shorter. A time will surely come when the 'moment-count' of my Yesterday's will be completed. My journey will have come to an end, here on this earth. And the opportunity for me to look toward Tomorrow will be no more. In other words, whenever my 'number' is up, Tomorrow will no longer be available to even consider.

William Shakespeare's character in 'Macbeth' understood the sobering reality of Tomorrow:

> "Tomorrow, and tomorrow, and tomorrow,
> Creeps in this petty pace from day to day,
> To the last syllable of recorded time;
> And all our yesterdays have lighted fools
> The way to dusty death.
> Out, out, brief candle!
> Life's but a walking shadow, a poor player
> That struts and frets his hour upon the stage
> And then is heard no more. It is a tale
> Told by an idiot, full of sound and fury
> Signifying nothing."

— Macbeth (Act 5, Scene 5, lines 17-28)

THE FACT that Tomorrow isn't a sure thing doesn't mean Tomorrow doesn't have an impact on our lives, however. Worry, anxiety, fear, doubt. They all have their foundations firmly rooted in Tomorrow. (I never worry about something that's already happened. I worry about what *might* happen ... Tomorrow.) I've noticed that the bible refers to 'tomorrow' many times, too, but usually it is in the context of God telling people what *He's* going to do 'Tomorrow.'

"If this happens today, then Tomorrow something else is going to happen," says God. Most of the time, in the bible, Tomorrow isn't a season of time; it's a date on the calendar that He points to, a date that's inextricably tied to Today. As soon as Today is finished, Tomorrow will be here.

Or will it?

Unless I'm God (and obviously I'm not, and neither are you,) Tomorrow isn't locked-in. Tomorrow isn't for sure. Tomorrow is a 'maybe,' at best. It's a proposal, of sorts. It's a day that may not ever get here. It *might* get here. I live my life as if I *know* it's a forgone conclusion that there will be a day following the day that I'm living; I assume there will be a Tomorrow in my life.

But, maybe not.

Terminally ill patients —those who have already been told by doctors that their time is running out— have a unique 'knowing,' I think. They've been told, in different words, of course, that the sun that sets on their Today may not rise for them ... Tomorrow. Whether we are actually aware of it or not, that's a reality we *all* have to deal with. As lyricist Sammy Lewis wrote, "Tomorrow may never come, for all we know." We're all terminal.

Knowing something isn't the same as paying attention to it, however. The sun came up this morning, for example. That's a fact. But I didn't give that reality a moment's notice. And, although I'm keenly aware of a truth — my life is short — I don't spend a lot of time worrying about just how short it might be. Instead, like most people I think, I walk through Every Day, living as if I know I've got at least one more Tomorrow left.

When one of my friends dies unexpectedly — a friend I just talked to Yesterday — I catch myself responding to their death as if it was 'totally unexpected.' Since I know everyone is terminal, and no one gets away from this life alive, why don't I *expect* it when people die? It's because I *assume* Tomorrow will arrive with the sunrise.

The Song Writer says that life is like a vapor: *"Indeed, You have made my days as handbreadths, And my age is as nothing before You; Certainly every man at his best state is but vapor.* (Ps. 39:5, NAS) Steam evaporates into thin air as quickly as it appears. And, in the grand scope and scheme of time and eternity, our lives come and then go in much the same way.

I would not for a moment suggest that we all become preoccupied with the fact that we're going to die, or that we fixate on or worry about Tomorrow's uncertainty. In fact, Tomorrow is the only *specific* day Jesus said we *shouldn't* worry about. In essence, he said we've got plenty to occupy our minds just thinking about Today, without letting our minds wander off into Tomorrow, that day that may not ever get here.

But how do I live my life Today, without thinking about Tomorrow? Why does it seem so logical to do things like plan budgets, or develop weekly schedules? Why do teachers write lesson plans for the week? What's the point of responsible adults preparing a will or a living trust, if there's no need to think about Tomorrow?

Even pastors, who are suppose to be reasonably familiar with the words of Jesus, seem to pay particular attention to a day called Tomorrow, in their professional lives, don't they? Every pastor I know spends much time thinking, (especially on Saturday nights,) about what they need to say on Sunday, when Tomorrow comes.

The answer to those questions is pretty obvious: There's a huge difference between not *thinking* about Tomorrow, and pretending that what may happen Tomorrow has no conse-quence. *"Be very careful, then, how you live—not as unwise but as wise, making the most of every opportunity, because the days are evil,"* says The Book. (Eph. 5:15,16 NIV) The wise person doesn't *ignore* Tomorrow; ignoring Tomorrow, or pretending God never mentioned such a day is not a wise thing to do.

No, I don't want to *ignore* Tomorrow. I just don't want to become so convinced that Tomorrow is a 'done deal' that I live it before it gets here.

Living Tomorrow before it gets here is about *assuming,* I think. I 'assume' things about Tomorrow that are not necessarily rooted in reality. For example, I assume I'll feel as good Tomorrow as I do Today. I've got a ton of stuff I need to do, Tomorrow. Pay bills. Get the mower fixed. I've got two trees to plant. I'll buy the trees at the nursery this afternoon. Then, first thing Tomorrow morn-ing, I'll plant them, unless ... unless I'm so sick, Tomorrow, that I can't lift my head from my pillow. In that case —(would that be a 'pillow case? Sorry, I couldn't resist.) —I guess planting the trees wouldn't work out. I just *assume* I'll feel as good Tomorrow as I do Today.

We all assume things. Perhaps that's the challenge of Tomorrow. Assuming there will be a Tomorrow is one thing; *presuming* upon Tomorrow's certainty... might be quite another.

If someone knocks on your door in the middle of the night, you don't 'assume' it's someone you know. You look through your door's peep hole to see who's there. But if your *neighbor* knocks on your door every night at exactly 6:30 pm, and the current time is 6:30, you *presume* the knock at your door is your neighbor, because she *always* comes over at precisely 6:30. 'Presume' is from the Latin *pre* "before" and *sumere* "to take," as in, 'taking something for granted.' I can easily (and even reasonably) assume there will be a Tomorrow. (After all, up to this point in time, hasn't there *always* been a Tomorrow?) But I need to guard against being *presumptuous* about Tomorrow, because that's a risky place to live.

WHEN OUR CHILDREN WERE SMALL, we had a tradition of sorts. Every Sunday evening, my wife would break out the waffle iron, and prepare batter. She'd slice bowls of different kinds of fruit, set the syrup on the table, along with several kinds of home-made jam she had canned herself. She'd set the jar of peanut butter on the table, too, just for me, because I like peanut butter on my waffles.

And most Sundays nights, we'd gather for waffle night, and enjoy conversation and the building of gorgeous waffles we woofed down with great alacrity. Our entire family benefitted from my wife's faithfulness and provision on waffle nights. Her loving preparations created wonderful and tasty food, coupled with warm and meaningful memories. My boys and I naturally came to *assume* that Sunday nights were waffle nights.

We *always* had waffles on Sunday nights.

But that is not to say that we were 'presumptuous.' I would never want my sons to presume upon the good and loving intentions of their mother. She didn't 'owe us' a waffle. We enjoyed the benefits of her love because she loved to make us happy. If we showed up at the kitchen table, plates and silverware in hand, waiting as if my wife was somehow duty-bound to cook for us, it would be most rude and presumptuous, indeed.

And I certainly don't want to *presume* upon God, either. God doesn't owe me another Tomorrow. Whether I will be granted another Tomorrow is known ... only to Him.

Tomorrow seems much too 'knowable' for a lot of people, I think, even though The Book says, no it isn't. James, the half-brother of Jesus, mentions how ignorant we really are about Tomorrow, when he writes, "You don't know what's going to happen tomorrow."

Tomorrow isn't for *sure*. And, have you read it lately? The writer of Hebrews wrote that "Jesus Christ is the same, yesterday, and today, and forever." (Heb. 13:8, NIV) But he says *nothing* about "yesterday, and today, and *Tomorrow*." Because His word tells me He is a faithful and good God, and because I have seen that provision in my life many times, I can *assume* that if I live to see Tomorrow, He will continue to faithfully provide for my life. In fact, every good and perfect gift comes from Him. He has been so faithful in my life that I can safely assume he will always be that way, since He is eternal and immutable.

But that is not to say I can safely presume that God's goodness *guarantees* I'll see Tomorrow. He has never obligated Himself with regard to how many Tomorrows I am entitled. He has only obligated Himself to my eternity. Jesus died and rose from the dead, so that my eternity could be secured.

Yes. Because of Jesus, eternity is a 'for sure' kind of word.

But Tomorrow? Not so much.

Tomorrow is a lot more ... *iffy*.

7

THE SEVENTH DAY

A DAY OF REST ... Forever.

"I have played the fool ..."

— KING SAUL, NEARING THE END OF HIS LIFE

"For we are his workmanship, created in Christ Jesus to do good works, which God prepared in advance for us to do."

— (EPH. 2:10, NIV)

"I wish it need not have happened in my time," said Frodo. "So do I," said Gandalf, "and so do all who live to see such times. But that is not for them to decide. All we have to decide is what to do with the time that is given us."

— J.R.R. Tolkien, Fellowship of the Ring, Second
Chapter, "The Shadow of the Past."

"The Israelites will keep the Sabbath, observe Sabbath-keeping down through the generations, as a standing covenant. It's a fixed sign between me and the Israelites. Yes, because in six days God made the Heavens and the Earth and on the seventh day he stopped and took a long, deep breath."'

— Ex. 31:17, The Message

I once knew a man named Caleb. A very nice man. Amiable. Warm and friendly with everyone he met. He lived in a little house in the country, a mile or two from town. That house where Caleb lived was in the mountains of Southern Tennessee, in a small community where people wave when they pass you on the street; a friendly place, where everybody seems to either be friends with, or related to everybody else.

And Caleb was a regular fixture in his tiny town.

He had a certain habit for which he was known. (A *ritual* was what it was.) His unusual morning ritual always included a ride to town. That would not have been particularly odd, except ... except that Caleb had no visible means of propulsion. No car he owned. Not even a bicycle to ride. No way to get from where he was to where he thought he might like to be.

And so, every morning, he stood along that road, in front of his little house, *thumbing* a ride.

Every Day, when he came out of his house, he would beg

a two-mile ride to town. Caleb hitchhiked. Like some school boy looking for the morning's bus. His arm stretched expectantly, Caleb would stand on the side of that road, out in front of his tiny house, his opposable right thumb pleading, hoping for a ride from whomever might be passing by. As cars approached, of course, Caleb often recognized the drivers. The people in his small community had grown accustomed to seeing his smiling face every morning as he stood in front of his tiny house, imploring people to stop and give him a ride to town.

But, even if he didn't know the person approaching, he waved, like he always did. He waited, like he always did. He watched expectantly for some compassionate driver who would have mercy on his plight, and give him a lift to town.

Something odd, though. As he stood, looking far down the way, waiting for a car to approach his side of the road, if he heard a car coming from the other direction? He was known to cross the road. Somedays, he would walk from one side of the road in front of his little house to the other side. He would point his opposable thumb *away* from his small town. Caleb would change directions.

And if that driver stopped to ask him where he might be going, Caleb had an interesting response: "Wherever."

I KNOW ANOTHER MAN, too: a man named '*me.*'

And every morning, he stands.

Waiting.

He looks down life's road.

He anticipates.

In anxious expectation, he hopes, and waits for a lift down some road toward his Ultimate Destination.

But what of the distant noise?

The sound of Heaven's Chauffeur approaching, going a *different* way.

If He pauses to ask *me* about my destination, and where He might take *me*,

I wonder?

Will I be purposeful and innocent in my response?

Will I be as wise as Caleb, and say ...

"Wherever?"

IF TOMORROW IS the only day Jesus said we shouldn't worry about, A Day of Rest represents the only day God said we should never forget. "Remember the Sabbath ..." said The Only God There Is, in His Book.

A Day of Rest stands unique from all the other days, in that it is the only day common to both God and the man He created.

None of the other days touch God the way they touch me. For example, God doesn't view Someday the way I do. (Now that I think about it, God doesn't view a lot of things the way I do. But I digress.)

God isn't affected by Somedays. He doesn't have a dream about what may happen, Someday, in His head, the way I do. He never *wonders* about a Someday that can seem so far off, as I do.

And He's never waiting around for something to come along or happen, Any Day (now) the way I do, either. He's never bored with the monotony of Every Day life. And God — great and awesome as He is — can't remember all the past sins and failures in my Yesterday, the way I do. Unlike me, when He forgives, He truly forgets about my Yesterday, burying my failures in that great sea of His forgetfulness and grace.

While Today, for me, is twenty-four hours long, Today for the Great I Am is eternally... now. It's always 'now' for God, never part of some Today, stuck between my Yesterdays and my Tomorrows.

And, what about Tomorrow? God never worries about what He already knows, and He already knows... everything. So God never worries. Whatever Tomorrow may contain (if it contains anything at all,) He's got it covered. So, He instructs in His Book that I spend no time worrying about Tomorrow.

But A Day of Rest?

A Day of Rest is the only day God said for me to specifically *remember;* the only day I share in common with the God of All the Universe. God had a Day of Rest, and He specifically instructed in His Book that I should have one, too.

When the God of All Time decided to wind the 'clock of days,' He declared a *beginning* to it all. "And there was evening, and there was morning. The first day," says The Book. And after the first day, there came a second, and third and another and another and another until God — the God of All Strength, Might, and Power — had evidently had enough. The Bible says that after He finished all his creating, working six full days making stuff like stars and fish and light and everything else that was, or ever would be created, He *rested*. He took a day off. He kicked back, He did. Looked at all He had made in the previous six days, and said, "This is good. It's all ... very good."

Yes, God looked at what went on in His six days of incredible creativity and noted that those were 'good days.' But then, he marked that seventh day as 'holy.' Think about it. God had six 'good' days in a row, before he declared, not a "good" day, but a *holy* day. (And, everybody knows there's a big difference between a *good* day and a *holy* day.)

Years later, when Moses walked up Mount Sinai to have a discussion with God, (well, actually, it wasn't as much a discussion as it was a 'laying down of The Law') God brought up that Day of Rest, again. "Remember the Sabbath," said God. And, He wrote it down in stone for Moses, and everyone else to read, so no one would have an excuse for forgetting: remember the Sabbath, because God said it was a holy day.

For certain, a Day of Rest includes physical, mental, emotional and spiritual renewal. Human beings need respite from physical labor in order to allow opportunity for the worship of the God of All Creation. Body, soul, and spirit are restored, as we worship Him.

And so, a Day of Rest is very important. God Himself told us to observe it; that day we set aside to pause, rest from all our labor of the previous six days, and take advantage of a holy opportunity to focus on, and converse with and worship The God Who Made Everything, The God Who Knows Everything, The God Who Has Us In Mind.

THERE ARE other ways to picture A Day of Rest, in addition to its being a specific day for personal renewal, important as that is. A Day of Rest can represent for some, an *arrival* point. It's more than just a 'day off,' or a break in life's normal routine. God's Book often mentions people 'resting and being buried with their fathers.' In such instances, A Day of Rest wouldn't just be a 'break in life's normal routine;' it would represent a cessation *from* routine, the day a person dies, the day an individual stops living. Every Day, in fact, pall bearers carry individuals to their final 'resting place' in some cemetery. Verses may be read. Songs may even be sung. Tears shed. Flowers adorn a casket that waits to be lowered to that 'final resting place.'

But the haunting reality is that most people believe 'final' doesn't mean *Finished*. We certainly do live our lives until we die, but then what? Well, then there must be an accounting before the God Who Said, "Remember."

And therein lies part of the challenge of a Day of Rest.

DR. CURT THOMPSON in his wonderful book, The Soul of Shame, wrote:

> "Of all the things that set us apart from the rest of creation, one thing stands out: we tell stories ... Whether we know it or not, and whether we intend to or not, we live our lives telling stories; in fact, we don't really know how to function and *not* tell them."

> — THE SOUL OF SHAME: RETELLING THE STORIES WE
> BELIEVE ABOUT OURSELVES, P.II

Because we're all storytellers, there is another reality that can prove to be problematic. Frederick Buechner mentioned it when he wrote that the two most devastating words in the English language are, "So what?"

And, the two *saddest* words that could ever describe a storied life are 'So what?', too.

As a storyteller, if I tell my story to some other soul, and their response is, "So what?" I failed as a storyteller. As a writer of words, if someone reads my book, and their only response is 'And your point was ...?' That's just another way of saying, "So what?" Evidence I haven't done a good job of writing.

The truth is: In living out and telling the story of our lives, the "So what?" really matters.

Even the songwriter David wondered. In that Thirty-Ninth Psalm, he wrote, "Lord, make me to know my end, and what is the measure of my days, that I may know how frail I am." (Ps. 39:4, NKJV) I think the older David got, the more aware he was that he might be approaching a "final" Day of Rest, that he didn't have a lot of time left.

In fact, on the day *anyone* is *born*, they don't have a lot of time left.

David understood that an entire lifetime isn't much time, really, to make sense of it all. *None* of us have much time to leave a mark, make a difference, live a Day-of-Rest-full-life. As he sat, (perhaps on some lonely shepherd hillside,) he admitted his own sense of frailty and insecurity to The God Who Created Him. David must have wondered, at least to some degree, about his own, "So what?" when he asked that pensive question of God: "What is man, that you are mindful of him?"

A lot of people have "So what?" questions today, I think. Census figures in 2014 numbered more than 75 million people in the United States in the Baby Boomer generation. That's a lot of people who are approaching their own, personal finish line; people who may be asking themselves 'meaning-in-life' kinds of questions. But on some level, and in some way, I think individuals in *all* generations wonder about how their lives measure up.

What kind of difference does my life make? What significant story am I telling with my life? What picture do others see or imagine, when they think of me? How am I known? How am I doing, compared with everyone else on this planet? And since life is short and I really don't have a lot of time left, what if I come to the end of my journey on this earth and still haven't answered those nagging questions about the 'so what' of my life? How do I respond to those questions that seem so unanswerable?

And … what if I should die, before I live?

SOMETIMES, when people come into my office, I can tell by the way they act that they are genuinely glad to see me. They smile. They pat my arm. They are warm, and friendly.

But sometimes, when friends come into my office, I can tell by the way they act that they have some kind of *need* in their lives, and they are glad that I can be there to listen, to hear. That's the way it was when *he* came into my office that day.

My friend sat down across from me. Cordial. Gregarious. He chatted about his golf game, and the weather, and 'how are you doing' kinds of things. But I knew something more important than the weather had brought him to my office.

He *told* me, then.

He announced, or pronounced: "My sister died, Yesterday."

I told him I was so sorry for his loss. I did not know he had a sister. I've known him a long time, but I thought he was an only child. He thanked me for my expression of condolence, and then asked me if I could speak at a memorial service for her.

"I know you didn't know my sister, but we just wanted to have a service for her," he said.

And so it was, that as we sat in the quiet of my office, he told me about ... *her.*

She contracted measles when she was just 18 months old, which caused severe psychological delays. My friend said his sister couldn't feed herself, or dress herself. She suffered from profound deafness, and could not respond, or communicate her wishes. For twenty-eight years, her parents did their best to meet her every need; a twenty-four-hour-a-day journey of love. But when the sister was twenty-nine, her father died, leaving the mother to shoulder all of the responsibilities and demands of constant care for such a needy soul.

The brave mother, now alone and widowed, eventually saw how it would be impossible for her to provide for her beloved daughter's needs. Reluctantly, she placed her daughter in a facility where she could receive appropriate care.

And that daughter— a grown woman, still a helpless child — remained there for several more years; she lived in that place of perpetual unawareness until she passed from this life. My friend said that as far as he knew, his sister never once recognized anyone around her. Never acknowledged their presence. Never winked. Never smiled. Not once, in all her life.

Over the course of my ministry, I've had lots of meetings with family members, informing me of their loss, and asking if I could speak at a memorial for their loved one; some soul I have never personally met.

During such meetings, I gather data on the life of the one now passed. I ask questions. Tell me of their faith? Tell me of their relationships, their passions, their accomplishments? What were they like? Give me some funny story, or some glimpse of who they were. What did their life contain and amount to, and 'count for'? But my conversation that day with my friend about his sister did not include much information about those kinds of 'tell-me-what-they-did-with-their-life' details. After several questions of my friend, and very few answers, I told him that I would be honored to speak, to serve his family and the memory of his sister.

But, behind my pastor-face hid a pastor-concern. I didn't know what I could possibly say about her 'story' and her life. This service had the potential for being very difficult.

(I must confess that, while I usually pray about the sermons I publicly deliver — messages I preach, or teachings I bring — I don't usually *pray* about memorials, or funeral services. I just, well, 'do' them. I prepare my notes. I say what I hope will bring encouragement and comfort to family and friends. But I don't usually *pray* over what I'm going to say at a memorial service. I don't think I've ever admitted that, before.)

But I spent a lot of time thinking and praying the next few days, trying to prepare for *that* memorial service. I asked God to help me describe and honor a life that was, in all honesty, difficult to even imagine, let alone describe. For, what does one say about a living soul, who although created in the image of God and of inestimable worth, lived an entire lifetime some would describe as "not worth living"? No awareness. No words said, nor attitudes reflected. No life-goals achieved. No hobbies. No passions. Nothing that resembles what we call ... Everyday *life.*

As I pondered and prayed my way through my preparations for that service, it occurred to me that perhaps some of the people attending the memorial would have a sense of 'relief' about this one who had now, finally and mercifully, died. Her sufferings over, the number of days allotted to her now completed, she had truly entered a place of 'final rest.'

But what of the *rest* of *them*? Those who would be listening to my voice that day? They, too, were living souls, created in the image of God, and of inestimable worth. How did *they* feel as they gathered to remember this woman whose life seemed to contain so few elements that could actually be ... remembered?

I choose to believe that God helped me with what I really needed to say to those who met for the celebration of that precious soul. And, when the appointed time came for me to speak, I rose to my feet, and this, in so many words, is what I said:

> "We're here today to celebrate the life of a very rare, special, blessed person. We have not come to rehearse our pity for one now gone.
>
> But that does not mean 'pity' has no place in this gathering.
>
> For as we celebrate her rare life and memory, we would do well to weigh carefully our own pitiful lives, and take advantage of our own rare opportunity: a chance to examine an obvious and poignant truth her journey demonstrates to all of us.

She spent her entire life unaware. She never had a need to be famous, to be "noticed," or known; no need to accomplish some great feat. She never spent even one day of her life striving for success. And, until her obituary appeared a few days ago, she never had a story written about her in any newspaper or magazine, never saw her name on any marquee.

And what about you? What great feat do you point to in your own life that you feel has eternal significance? What secret wish hides just beneath the surface of your longing heart? A longing to be noticed or appreciated or understood?

She never suffered from that kind of longing.

Unlike all of us, she never heard a human voice because she was deaf. And she could not speak. Never once in her entire life did she ever form a word, or utter a word, or even hear the sound of her own voice.

And you? How many words have you heard in your lifetime that you wish you had never heard? Biting words. Hurting words. Words spoken to you, in some "Yesterday" of your life — words you wish to God you had never heard — or perhaps even more sadly, words you wish to God you had never ... said? Dumb words, spoken in the deafness of your un-hearing life; words you cannot retrieve or take back; pronouncements and declaratives you cannot expunge from your memory. What's the reckless 'word-count' for your life?

Her biting word-count?

Zero.

It is true that she never got to dress up for some fancy cotillion. No handsome prince ever came to her door to take her to a ball. In fact, she never once got to walk to her own closet to decide what to wear for a simple, Every Day activity. But then, how many days have you felt like you were merely going through the motions, dressing your weary life for yet another day of ... weary life?

Her earthly journey has been completed. How easy it would be to look at her life and feel sorry for her because of all she missed. She never spoke, she never heard, she never ... 'knew.' And yet, I ask you? When we closely examine her life, does it not demonstrate a poignant model of true meaning and purpose for us all?

For at the moment of her death, I wonder what it must have been like for her to cross from 'here' ... to 'Eternity'? What was it like to no longer be encumbered by the physical limitations she had known Every Day of her life. To be able to walk — for the very first time — and step unencumbered onto Heaven's Great Stage. What must it have been like for her recognize Someone for the very first time; to have the first face she ever really 'knew' be the very Countenance of God? And the very first words she would ever understand? The very first words she would hear, spoken by a loving, caring, all-knowing God?

'Welcome Home.'

Thank God for this child of His, who spent her entire life without ever recognizing a face, or hearing a word, or even having a casual conversation with a friend. I for one, have not come today to say goodbye to a pitiful soul. Rather, I choose to hear Today what her life has actually spoken. In this life, it is true that she never learned to talk. But does that mean she didn't speak? No. No, as we gather here to celebrate, we need to rejoice and be grateful for just how loudly and powerfully her blessed life has spoken to us all, without her ever uttering a word.

The person who cannot hear the lessons to be learned from observing a journey like hers ... is a person to be most pitied, indeed."

～

EVERYONE KNOWS a sad story about some young child just beginning life who dies, suddenly. It is a fact of life: No matter how young an individual may be, they're old enough to die. And, conversely, no matter how much of life an individual may have 'wasted,' or squandered, or messed up, or 'lived,' even if they're older than dirt, if they're still breathing and kicking — if they've still got the ability to think and act in a coherent fashion — they've still got time to 'redeem their time.' They're young enough to start finishing well. We're all young enough, no matter our age, to begin to live a life that truly matters. Everyone is old enough to die, and young enough to live.

Annie Dillard mentioned some of what I see as the challenge of successfully living out A Day of Rest in her book on the craft of writing, *The Writing Life.* She noted that there are a lot of similarities between living and writing, and suggested that to be successful at writing, an author needed to write as if he or she were *dying.* And the 'target audience' for the writing? Terminal patients. She asked would-be writers,

> "What would you begin writing if you knew you would die soon? And what could you possibly say to a dying person that would not enrage by its triviality."

> — ANNIE DILLARD, THE WRITING LIFE, P.68

One of the questions an editor friend asked me, the first time I approached him about publishing my book was, 'Who's my reader?' Successful books should have a target audience, of course, and writers would do well to know and understand that audience. I flinched at telling my editor friend that my target audience was terminal people, and that I was a dying man writing to dying people.

But Annie Dillard would say that's exactly what's happening, when I try to define and examine A Day of Rest. I'm not sick, right now. In fact, I'm in great health. But that doesn't mean I'm not 'terminal'. I'm a terminal guy, writing to 'terminal' people, hoping printed words encourage other souls in their journey and search for meaning and purpose. Everyone has read how-to books filled with trivialities and mindless simplicities about such things.

The challenge, then: How to define a life lived and finished well? How shall I live a life where I truly feel at rest with myself and who I am, at rest with my God and my walk with Him, and at rest with those I encounter Every Day, in the important relationships in my life?

A Caring Relationship With God …

Deep and meaningful life at it's core, is *relational,* I believe. And there are only three totally unique relationships that I am aware of: There's a relationship with God, a relationship with myself, and a relationship with those I encounter along my journey here on God's earth.

It stands to reason that discovering real meaning in life begins by knowing the Creator of All My Days, and being in relationship with Him. Eugene Peterson paraphrased the words of the Savior in Matthew's gospel, when he wrote, "… *Come to me. Get away with me and you'll recover your life. I'll show you how to take a real rest. Walk with me and work with me—watch how I do it. Learn the unforced rhythms of grace. I won't lay anything heavy or ill-fitting on you. Keep company with me and you'll learn to live freely and lightly.*" (Matt. 11:28, The Message)

God is a relational Sovereign who loves company. He must love walking and talking, too. He created an idyllic setting in the Garden of Eden, where He could walk and talk with the man He intended to create. He had no 'picture' to go by, as He pondered what a man should look like. After all, He'd never made a man before.

"I know," said the Infinitely Creative God. "I'll make *him* look like *Me*."

And so, He did. He took dust from the earth and formed and fashioned a man in His own image; a man He would love. He breathed into that man His own, holy breath, and at that very moment in time, man became a living soul. Then, God placed that man, Adam, into the middle of the Garden He had created just for the two of them.

He began conversing with Adam, as if he were the only guy in the world. Of course, at that time, Adam *was* the only guy in the world. But, the Relational God of Creation, The Only God In The Universe (or anywhere else, for that matter,) noticed something. He said to himself, "It's not *good* that man should be alone, that man should be the only human." He decided that man, too, should be in relationship, not only with God himself, but with other human beings.

And so, The Great Physician 'operated.' He caused Adam to sleep like a baby (before there even was such a thing as a baby,) and skillfully removed Adam's rib, closing up the wound. Then, He made a 'fashion statement," of sorts. He *fashioned* that rib into ... *her;* that woman, that "Eve".

And that evening, Adam had Eve to talk to, and share life with, and yes, ... *know.* But God and Eve weren't the only two Adam became acquainted with.

He somehow showed up, too.

That serpent. That trickster, and liar, and thief. When Satan appeared on the scene, he wanted to know what God had been saying to Adam and Eve. "Did God *really* say that?" he asked. "Did God really say, 'You must not eat ...?'" And Eve said, "Yes. He really said that. We can't eat from *that* tree, or even touch it, or we'll die."

Die? An interesting concept, when you actually think about it. I mean, how would Adam and Eve know dying would be so bad? They'd never known anyone who had actually died before, after all. And besides, Satan had an answer to their reluctance.

"You won't die," said the liar.

Perhaps you know the rest of their story. They did eat. And at that very moment, they did know the difference between good and evil. They realized that they were no longer 'good' enough, that they should be ashamed of themselves for what they had done, ashamed of themselves because they were naked as picked birds. Because they had brought shame on themselves, they now knew and understood that they were in deep trouble with God, and they looked for a safe place to hide.

But the relational God had never planned to provide a place for 'hiding' in the Garden or the universe He had created. God's great intention was that He would be *known*, not hidden from. He had perfectly designed His world for walking, and talking and enjoying an incredible One-on-one relationship with man. Now, that kind of relationship was lost. Adam and Eve realized their guilt. And it surely must have caused them a great and irreversible sorrow. They saw that their disobedience and their naivety in believing a lie had now created an impenetrable wall between God and human flesh. A barrier now existed; one so wide and high and long and deep that it was impossible to scale. Man would not only have to *earn* his living by the sweat of his brow; from that moment on, man would have to 'earn' his way back into God's good graces.

Yet, no matter how hard man worked, no matter how much he tried to 'do good', or 'be good,' he would never be good enough. He would never know a Day of Rest from his striving. His self-doubt would plague him; his inadequacy would serve as a constant reminder of his failure at living up to God's righteous demands. Regardless of how earnestly he toiled, he could never 'finish well.' He could never be 'done' and deserving of a Day of Rest from his sin, and his striving to earn God's favor.

Sinless perfection is God's standard for relationship. Tragically, because of his disobedience, human kind would never again share a Holy-day with the Holy God, unless ... unless a Remedy could be provided. Our Relational God's deep and eternal desire to make Himself known once-and-for-all to humanity, prompted Him to respond to man's rejection with His own, amazing provision. Through His grace and love, the Relational God provided the only way a person could know a rest-filled life.

He sent His son.

Like His Father who once walked with Adam in the Garden, God's only son, Jesus, now joyfully walked among men, conversing with them as One Man does to another. He taught. He healed. He loved. And then He offered Himself as the Perfect Sacrifice. He not only died for the sins of the world, He rose again!

And belief and acceptance of this gift of His loving sacrifice and forgiveness for sin, once again provided the potential access to relationship with the God of All Our Days. By trusting in Christ's atoning death, man could finally cease his 'working' to please God, and realize that now, for all eternity there would remain a 'Sabbath-rest for the people of God.' (Heb. 4:9, NIV)

The first 'foundation stone,' then, for living a rest-filled life is being in a right relationship with The Relational God, by accepting the free gift of His forgiveness for all our sins. Because I have known and experienced that forgiveness for myself, even though I am keenly aware of my own "temporariness" in this world, I rest confident of His watchful presence, knowing He takes joy and notice of my every step and way.

My wife told me of a man she encountered at the mall one day. Her noticing had a profound impact on her. She observed the man as he shopped. He seemed to be looking for just the right 'something'. He flipped through racks of shirts, and pants, and jackets and sweaters. He didn't hurry. He didn't seem to worry. He just looked and shopped and ... wheeled.

He wheeled himself around that large store. He wasn't disabled, mind you. (We dislike that word at our house.) No. He was *different*-abled, and his only way to get around was his wheelchair. My wife marveled at his skill in moving his chair in and out of the rows of clothing. She watched him reach and stretch for items. She noticed him a bit later, too, taking the items he had selected to the clerk for payment.

But watching the man shop was not what caused her to be impacted by his life. It was what she read as he was leaving the store, and making his way down the mall; just a small sign, carefully lettered and attached to the back of his wheelchair, placed there for the benefit and education of all who cared to observe it. The sign read:

"I may not be perfect, but parts of me are excellent."

A worthy mantra for fellow pilgrims on their way toward living out a Day of Rest, and finishing well.

A Caring Relationship With Myself ...

If life is relational at its core, (and I'm convinced it is,) well then, besides knowing a caring and personal relationship with my God, the one person I'm also going to have to be in an authentic and genuine relationship with is *me*. I have to settle-in on a 'caring relationship' with myself, and who I am. That can be a problem.

I think human beings come factory-installed with a tremendous need to *hide*, not only not from God, but from ourselves as individuals, and from all those other people who may be watching our lives. I chafe at the idea of slowing down to think about who I am, too much. I want the volume of noise in my life to drown-out what I'm actually thinking about *me*. Dietrich Bonhoeffer said that we human beings chase ourselves from one activity to the next so we don't have to spend any time alone with ourselves, looking at ourselves in the mirror.

Man, do I believe that! Maybe it's that 'looking at myself in the mirror' that caused me to notice, again, something I've known for a long time.

I AM PORTLY, or stout. In fact, I'd have to admit that I'm downright corpulent. If you saw me, you might use *another* word to describe what you see when you see me, of course. I know that word, too. I see the evidence of it when I look in my mirror after a shower. It's that short word. Three letters long. But I don't let myself use that word, when I think of *me*, because, well, if I were to use *that* word, I would have to acknowledge that I'm overweight. 'Portly' feels a bit more comical to me; 'stout' isn't too damaging to my self-esteem, either. So I admit it. I'm portly. I'm stout. I'm downright corpulent.

I do not give myself 'permission,' please understand. I certainly don't excuse my lack of self-control. Over the years, I have continually wrestled with *me* over my weight. Up to this point in time, I've lost nearly every match. There have been victories, of sorts, for periods of time. And, I still tell myself I have hope of winning the battle permanently, of course. But so far, I have yet to overcome being portly. Why, I wonder, do I shy away from that other word, though? What's so 'bad' about using that other word to describe *me*? The cause or reason for the way I *am* isn't a mystery, after all. I consume more calories than I burn. That's an obvious truth. And it's been that way for a long, long time.

I don't like to think much about my corpulence, though. And so, like Adam of old, I hide my nakedness as soon as I can. Every Day, after I've taken my shower, and noticed in that brutally honest mirror that I continue to fail in winning my battle with food and exercise, I leave that lonely bathroom. Without a comment to myself, I walk to my closet. I search for something to wear that will hide my unspoken and personal failure; my disappointment with ... *me*.

I took an unusual risk one day several months back to describe what I had been feeling with a doctor friend. I told him that I had noticed that I focus much of my life and energy 'outwardly.' People come to me for counsel. Doctors come to me for coaching. Virtually all of my interactions with others revolve around *them* and their need. I admitted that I wasn't good at being transparent with others about my own needs, and that I struggled to allow others to bring nurture or help into my life. I have many people around me who love me, and I know would readily provide encouragement for me. I told my doctor friend that on those rare instances when I make a feeble attempt at being transparent, and share a personal need with someone who cares about me, I've noticed something strange.

I'm so use to 'giving out' that when others try to 'pour in' to my life, almost seamlessly and without even noticing it most of the time, I reverse the polarity of the conversation. I turn the table. I adroitly cause the focus to switch from *me,* and my need ... to *them*. I start talking about their life, their need, their struggle. They willingly allow such transitions, because everyone, I suppose, needs someone who will listen to their life, and ... care. The result of my turning this 'invisible table' is that, often, I have an unmet need in my own life; a real need for comfort or encouragement.

I admitted to my doctor friend that I have skillfully taught myself to nurture *myself* with food; when my emotional and spiritual batteries feel drained, to recharge, I may eat something, even though I'm not particularly hungry.

It was difficult for me to risk sharing my observation with my friend. I have great respect for him, and his response to me brought both clarity and truth in an unsuspected way.

He said, "What you need is a good Jesuit in your life."

"A Jesuit?" I said. "Why on earth would I need a Jesuit?"

"Because," he continued, "if you tried to 'turn the tables' on a Jesuit, he would stop you, and tell you, 'This isn't about me; it's about you.'"

"Where do you find a good Jesuit when you need one?" I asked.

I mean, I'm a Protestant guy. I've never understood or learned much about cloistered people. And everyone knows that the very word, 'Jesuit' sounds cloistered, doesn't it? Why would I need to go talk to someone who's living a cloistered life?

And then, it occurred to me.

In a very real way, I *am* living a cloistered life. I'm the one who is cloistered. My life is shut tight, so no one can see through the windows of my inner man. I'm so protective of the *me* on the other side of those windows that I even fail to acknowledge who I am. I am more than a three-letter word. My identity and my value have been established by the God who has always had *me* in mind. I struggle with the very idea of care for *me*, or celebrating *me.*

What else might I see if I took the time to actually look in that morning mirror? What do I notice about *me*? What do I affirm as 'true' about the *me* who is created in the image of God?

And what might I be saying about *me* that isn't true at all?

Poet Marilee Zdenek wrote a wonderful piece describing how a lot of people feel, in her collection, "Splinters in my Pride:"

Long ago, I asked my parents, (using other words)
"Am I of value? Does my life have meaning?"
Then I asked my teachers, later, directors and editors,
husband and friends—
"Am I of value? Does my life have meaning?"
Then I asked God and God said "Yes."
And That should have finished it.
But it didn't.

John Stott wrote that it was his conviction that our heavenly Father says the same thing to us Every Day: "My dear child, you must always remember who you are." I believe he's right. I have to always remember who I am. I don't want to be like the double-minded man James talks about, in The Book. I don't want to look in some mirror, see the real *me*, and then walk away and find a hiding place so I can't be known for who I am. For *me* to live a rest-filled life, for me to finish well, I need to have a saving relationship with Jesus, of course. But I've got to be okay with caring about *me*, too.

I've got to courageously confess and acknowledge a huge identity lie: I lied to you moments ago, when I told you, "I am portly." I'm not portly, or stout. I'm not even corpulent, or that other word I never like to use. No. I'm Ken, and all that that means. Portly may be how I look; but it's not who I am.

I am 'God's handiwork.' (Eph. 2:10) I will never live a rest-filled life by attaching labels to myself, (or allowing others to do so!) or by accepting the lie that my failures define my person-hood. I surely will fail, in many ways, as a parent. I fail as a husband. I even fail as I manage my failures, fail to trust God, fail to trust others who could speak their life into my life. If I'm going to have an honest relationship with myself, I'd be disingenuous, dishonest, and downright foolish to ignore my failures, pretending they never happened. I *care* about my failures. I will continue to wrestle with my own flesh, Every Day. I want to grow in my ability to address my failures, too.I will never give myself permission to stop contending with myself.

But I will never capitulate and surrender in allowing those failures to define *me*. I belong to the God who cares about *me*; the God who is the author of my significance. My friend, Richard Swenson got it right in his great book on contentment, when he wrote: 'We dare not label our work, our lives, our kids, our churches, or our world as failures until God pounds the gavel."

No. I am not disabled.

I am different-abled. In fact, on some level, we're all different-abled. Truth is, there's only one "*us*" on the face of this earth. We are all, — as Adam of old— one-of-a-kind, custom-made-by-God individuals. How rest-filled life would be, if we could live Every Day accepting a certain and absolute reality: If I have a right relationship with God, I am a 'new creation' on the inside, perfect in God's eyes.

And on the outside? Well, I may not be perfect, ... but parts of me are excellent.

God said that, too.

And that should have settled it.

But it didn't.

Must be those awful mirrors.

A Caring Relationship With You

We've probably never met, you and I. As you read these words, you have no idea what my life is *really* like, what I had for breakfast this morning, what the room looks like where I now sit to write. If we passed each other on the way to our jobs, we wouldn't honk or wave at each other. We don't *know* each other, after all. And tonight, if we both stopped on the way home from work to pick up something for dinner, as we stood in line together at the check-out stand in the grocery store, you might notice that I had corn flakes and pork chops in my basket. You might even see a mousetrap or celery root, and wonder, "*What in the world?*"

But you probably wouldn't ask me, would you?

And if we stood together in that line at the market, as I placed my groceries on that black conveyor that moves mysteriously toward the clerk and his scanner, isn't it true? Isn't it true that one of us would eventually reach for that rubber divider at the checkout stand and place it between our groceries? After all, there mustn't be any confusion about where my life ends and yours begins. I don't want you to pay for my "stuff," and I certainly don't want to pay for yours.

But finding meaning and purpose, and a truly restful life while I'm still on this earth isn't like going to the store for a loaf of bread. I believe we 'terminal ones' can find that place of deepest joy, peace, and fulfillment by intentionally investing in caring relationships with those around us, Every Day.

But how does that kind of investment happen?

What can my storied life say to you? And, what word shall you leave with ones like me, when we meet along life's path? What advice shall you give me that will not enrage me by its triviality? What shall I tell you about how to be happy, as we stand in line at the grocery store? Shall I say, "Do as I do, and you will be happy?" Or what of contentment? Shall I give you five secrets, or quote you five bible verses to memorize so that you can have contentment?

I know. I know what I could leave with you. I could tell you of the many setbacks in my life, and what I learned about over-coming, and being victorious, and successful. I could give you hints on ways to face your challenges head-on, and how to change the plot line in your own narrative. I could warn you of the terrible diseases of 'performance,' and 'perfectionism.' I could tell you that there is no known remedy for those twin plagues, apart from the curative power of God and His loving grace.

No. I will not give you lists. You are a dying patient, like me, after all. Your time is as short as mine for hearing pointless and empty words that go nowhere. What could possibly be the *answer* to living a Day of Rest-full life that impacts others? I have come to the conclusion that the best way for me to express my *care* for those around me Every Day, is not to provide *answers* to the tough questions in life. That would, indeed, be pointless. Instead, I choose to *have* no answers. Only questions.

I will tell you what I mean.

I HAVE a friend who often reminds me that "Life is a giant pain machine." I've known that truth for a long time, but his wise perspective gives me permission to admit what I already know: Life is pain-filled, and finding a Day of Rest in the midst of the pain isn't a job for sissies.

I know. I've heard them, too. Those well-meaning and seem-ingly bright, mature believers who throw out misquoted bible verses they've 'memorized' to explain the inexplicable. When a deep trial comes to someone they care for, they pull out a ridiculous comment, as if it were a one-size-fits-all-answer for just such an occasion: "Remember. The bible says, 'God will never give you more than you can bear.'"

Say what? Where? Show me in The Book where it says that. (I suspect it's in the same chapter as "The Lord helps those who help themselves." As of this writing, I have yet to discover either quote in any of the dozen or so translations of scripture in my library.)

No. The bible most certainly does *not* say God will never give me (or anyone else) more than we can bear. I've had many times in my life when my knees have buckled and life's unexpected circumstances have driven my face into a blackness I felt I could never come out of.

My wife, Randee, and I have been married for a long time. And for most of those years, she's been afflicted with a degenerative disc disease that has caused her a gnawing and deep pain, virtually Every Day of our married lives. She's had five fusion surgeries in her back and neck. She's had the joints in *both* sides of her jaw replaced ... three times! She's had both knees replaced, numerous hand and foot surgeries. My wife and I have known and experienced what my friend Bill has correctly given definition to: Life is a giant pain machine.

You, for certain, have your own giants, your own experiences, drawn from those moving parts of your own pain machine. We all know real *life,* and sometimes that reality begs description. Answers to the 'Why-did-this-happen-to-me?' question virtually never come. And even *if* some well-meaning friend tried to answer that mysterious question, I wouldn't accept their answer. Probably you wouldn't either. No one truly knows the answer to that question, after all. No one but God. (And He's not saying; at least not so I can hear.)

Everyone has had events or seasons and times in their lives when a *caring* God was hard to imagine, or see, or perhaps even believe in; seasons when God seemed to be testing, or trying, or hiding or leading in a way that either wasn't clear, or was totally unacceptable to us. St. Ignatius of Loyola defined sin as "an unwillingness to trust that what God wants is our deepest happiness." When I use that definition of sin, I have no problem confessing: I am a sinner.

I cannot count the times in my life when I felt certain I knew better than God what I needed for my own happiness and fulfillment, and I was convinced God was out to keep me from what I wanted. Each of those times, I was both wrong, and I was right. I was wrong to think He didn't know what was best for me. And I was right in assuming He wasn't about to give in to my near-sighted desires. During those seasons of confusion or wondering, what I need most is another *caring* soul; a Jesuit-type (without the hooded frock), who, like me, is a novice at 'being still' and 'knowing He is God,' but can provide friendship and brotherhood along the way.

God said it a long time ago: It's not good that man should be alone. Being in a place of caring relationship with others — reaching out, walking alongside, encouraging those seeking perspective and a Day of Rest in the midst of storm — represents a huge piece in the puzzle of what it means to be human, and a child of the relational God. It is perhaps a mystery that when I reach out in a caring way to someone who crosses my path, I fulfill one of life's greatest challenges: living a life that is eternally meaningful.

Living a Meaningful 'So What?' Life

Thomas Merton wrote, "Ask me not where I live, or what I like to eat. Ask me what I am living for, and what I think is keeping me from living fully for that."

I've already said that I don't have a lot of answers to life's mysteries. But I do have questions. And so, I will ask you: As you reflect back on your life, and as you imagine moving forward from this Today —this very place you find yourself— What are you living for, and what might be keeping you from living fully for that?

Knowing the answer to those two questions seems paramount for me, if I am to experience true rest in my life on a daily basis. Several years ago, now, I decided to record my own, personal 'Credo and Purpose" statement; a 'what- am-I-living-for?' document. I now use it as a sort of touchstone to help me remember what I believe represents a meaningful life for *me*. I share it, in the hope that perhaps you, too, might spend time thinking about and defining your own 'purpose,' or belief about life's meaning for you:

A CREDO and Life Purpose Statement
For Ken Jones

My singular focus:

"I have determined to live my life to the glory and honor of Jesus Christ, with integrity, transparency and genuineness."

> *"But life is worth nothing unless I use it for doing the*
> *work assigned me by the Lord Jesus—the work of*
> *telling others the Good News about God's mighty*
> *kindness and love." (Acts 20:14, The Living Bible)*

My Hope:

When I die, as those who know me best are thinking of words to describe me — as they try to come up with some "one-word

epitaph" to carve on my tombstone—I would hope that among
the words that might come to mind would be the word ... REAL.

> — "AND WE, WHO WITH UNVEILED FACES ALL
> REFLECT THE LORD'S GLORY, ARE BEING
> TRANSFORMED INTO HIS LIKENESS WITH EVER-
> INCREASING GLORY, WHICH COMES FROM THE
> LORD, WHO IS THE SPIRIT." (2COR. 3:18)

My Responsibility

I. I will strive to demonstrate (by the way I live my life Every
Day) that I am committed to this inviolate principle: Life in the
Kingdom of God is defined by right relationships. Because I
believe that truth ...

- I will endeavor to cultivate my right relationship with
  God through His Son, Jesus, by communing daily,
  and serving wholeheartedly.
- I will endeavor to cultivate a right relationship with
  my "self," by submitting to the grace of God every
  day, allowing His penetrating forgiveness to
  strengthen me and heal me in both the healthy and
  broken areas of my life.
- I will endeavor to cultivate right relationships with
  those around me, as I submit myself to others for
  their instruction and encouragement, and as I serve
  as a teacher, encourager and mentor to those who
  cross my path.

II. I will strive to fulfill the two greatest commandments: I
will love God, and I will love people ... Every Day of my life.

III. I will strive to be a good steward of what I believe to be my two primary giftings from God, in order to invade and affect my world for Jesus Christ:

i. **Influence** — (Salt and Light – Matt. 5:13,14)

- I will influence my family, by serving them and encouraging them.
- I will influence those around me by coaching, modeling, teaching and mentoring at every opportunity.
- I will influence my world by answering God's clarion call to be a seasoning agent in the culture in which I find myself.
- I will make a consistent effort to intentionally touch and leave the fingerprints God has given me on the lives of those I come in contact with, because I am convinced that in Kingdom Life, there are no appointments that are not Divine. All my moments belong to Him.

2. **Creativity** — (God's workmanship, created in Christ Jesus to do good works – Eph. 2:10) I will demonstrate God's incredible imagination by joining Him, in creating expressions of His greatness and grace, through what I write, and what I say, and the work that I am privileged to do for Him.

IV. In all I say and do, I will attempt to hold "everyday life" up to the Light of Jesus Christ, so that other ordinary people like me, who watch my daily struggles and victories, might know and experience an extraordinary God, as they observe Him changing me (transforming me) into His own likeness, through His amazing Grace.

V. I will give myself one piece of daily advice: "Don't take yourself too seriously."

"For by the grace given me I say to every one of you: Do not think of yourself more highly than you ought, but rather think of yourself with sober judgment, in accordance with the measure of faith God has given you." (Rom.12:3, NIV)

SOMEDAY, the number of my days on this earth will have come to an end. But until that time, I will rest and delight in His 'wherever' path and destination for me, knowing that being 'grownup' and being mature and well-lived are not the same. We have no control over the 'quantity' of our days. But the 'quality' of life we live will be determined by our three great opportunities for relationship: A right relationship with God, an accurate and transparent relationship with ourselves, and a loving, *touch-ing* relationship with those we encounter along the way.

I have come to appreciate a great reward and opportunity; His open invitation to talk to God on a daily basis. Some of what I have been discussing with Him lately revolves around my walk to the 'finish' line, and how I'm feeling, these days. My dialogue often goes something like this:

> *May I know what a mature life really means, Lord.*
> *Help me define what it means to be well-lived, and*
> *then live my life to that definition.*

> *Some days. I feel my age.*
> *Some days, I just 'know' I'm getting older.*
> *Every time I stand up, it seems,*
> *My painful back tells me.*
> *I look into that morning mirror.*
> *I see my wrinkled brow, and I notice,*
> *again Every Day:*

I suspect, perhaps, that I'm not getting old.
I'm already there.

I'm not sure when 'getting old' starts. You would know
the answer to that question, Lord.
Life's beginning, and middle, and end were all known
and "scripted" by your good hand.
And my measly bit part in that script must surely be
approaching a final 'curtain call,' I would think.
Not Today, perhaps.
Maybe not even this year or next.
But in that grand scheme of yours — that 'Wherever?'
plan for me that you have known all along —
It can't be too many days or weeks or months or years,
Before my 'time' will have come.
I'm one of the old ones, now.
And I know the end surely is in sight.
As I approach my 'finish line,'
It's too late for accolades or notice of adoring fans.
But then, your grace assures me; your love
convinces me:
I can be confident of your smile and approval;
applause from the Audience of One.
May I be content with my station and place in this
journey, now, Lord;
May I quietly take my seat at life's learning
table, as one of the "old ones,"
Busying myself daily with your good and creative
work, while I wait for your sweet, beckoning call.
Agatha Christie wrote that she lived '... on borrowed
time, waiting in the anteroom for the summons
that will inevitably come."
I guess all of us live on that borrowed time, don't we?

We all live in that crowded anteroom,
Waiting for the inevitable (and unavoidable)
summons.
Life lived well is no game, for certain.
More like a drama on some temporal stage.
I can only trust that my part on that stage has been
well-played.
My lines delivered with conviction,
My scars earned through years of struggle,
and rehearsal and contending with life's
improvisational theatre.
May I be clothed, Today, Lord, not with some
ornamental costume of 'pretend' or impersonation.
Rather, may I be wrapped securely in the only
robe that matters: your loving righteousness.
Yes, I guess I'm one of the old ones, now.
Help me finish my part in life's drama by acting my
age, will you?
Because I have travelled miles, and heard the music of
life's storied song,
I should be at a place in my journey where
people notice things about me; things like
character, and wisdom, and love; things that truly
matter.
Time's march and its effect on my body are
easy to see, now, I suppose.
But, I wonder?
Can the same be said of my character and my
thinking?
We mature ones need to act our age.
We need to deport ourselves before others in
a way that causes them to take notice of the God

we have known; the God who has walked with us,
    along the way.
        Time has surely seasoned our many
    seasons, and our short path toward Your finish
    line, Your Day of Rest.
To be older and hopefully, wiser, is an honorable
    thing, I think.
And I'm convinced ... I'm one of the old ones, now.
May I be the kind of maturing and seasoned man who
    acts his age, Today.

SAIL ON, then, O fellow pilgrim. May you never stop dreaming about what may come along, Someday. And may what you're waiting for, Any Day (now) be exactly what God wanted to give you. May, Every Day, life have meaning and purpose for you. May the scars of your Yesterday bring to mind God's faithful attention to your struggles. May whatever remains of Today — the day you're actually reading these words — be filled with moments of your intentionally touching those around you, leaving fingerprints on those God brings your way. May you give no heed or worry to a Tomorrow that may never arrive. And may you, from this very moment in time, live-out a Day Filled With Rest and dependence on The God of All Our Moments.

    Kj

EPILOGUE

Pax Vobiscum

Just now, I watched Today begin.

Daybreak successfully chased that starred and starry
blackness called night from one side of this earth
to the other.
Only moments ago, the sun came up, and morning's
light finally ended what the dark had been up to
all night long.
Now, I sit listening to quiet fields. I hear
meadowlarks clearing their throats in the
distance, ready to join the chorus of a million
ordinary songs.
And, without missing a beat, the faint sound of
habitual things begins to drum on the yawning
dawn of this innocent day.
As that distant sun slowly begins to etch gray and
shadowed images across the horizon, and such
lovely landscapes as these,

I notice trees, their limbs casting mirrored shadows,
*   drawn upon the waiting ground.*
Spring leaves splay their ribbed palms, and force light
*   to draw down and give way.*
(For, light, once forced aside, must resign to shadowed
*   absence, you know.)*
Today's morning canvas waits, unframed and ready
*   for the Painter to begin;*
As yet untouched by mortal hands, Today awakens at
*   His bidding, and now, takes its form and meaning*
*   from the stroke of His brush and pen, and touch.*
If I keep watch, Today, will I see?
Will I notice the Maker of Heaven and Earth as He
*   moves heaven and earth?*

Will I don that cloak of servanthood's many colors?
Will I pledge allegiance again, Today, to the Sower as
*   He sews men's dreams and weaves time's*
*   tapestry?*
If I listen, will I hear?
Will I hear the lustral sound of that Sapient Word,
*   fresh, and inviting as a Living Stream?*
Or will my deaf ear turn away and join the noisome
*   silence of this shadowed world, feinting life while*
*   ignoring The Light?*

I know full well that Light shines in the darkness.
But the darkness has not understood it.
And as Today unfolds, even in the midst of the
*   brightness and knowing of His light, mystery's*
*   shadows fall upon my sorry soul;*
Yes, the silhouettes of life's many and storied
*   challenges lengthen, plotting, hoping to finally*

envelop and overwhelm that vacuous place and
space called "me."

With resolved resignation, I declare it:

Move on, O sun.
Make your patient way across the clutter of this time
and this space ... and this world.
Your roaming around God's heaven causes the
darkness to flee before you; you bring the light and
chase the night.
By your mere and gracious arrival, O sun, you bring a
freshness to the monotony of each and Every Day.

And with awe-filled resolution, I say it:
Move on, O Son.
You who are greater than any sun or its risings;
quietly now, slip into the disordered and
discordant confusion of this time and this space ...
and this, "me."

Yes, move on, Today, O sun.

And move on my "Today," O Son.
Move on me.
Find for me a Day of Rest.
And in that finding, take your leisure.

For, I already know.
I've known it all along.
After Today has closed, another cloaked and starry
blackness called night will return.
Or will it?

Who knows? Perhaps, before Tomorrow's dawn
comes, that night will arrive when no man
can work.

One day, some Someday will arrive; time will be
no more.
And your final *Day of My Rest will arrive.*
Yes, I will receive my summons to stand all alone in
that anteroom and wait;

Wait for You, my Maker, my Only Reward, You in
whom I live, and move, and have my being ... for
all Eternity.

Kj

ABOUT THE AUTHOR

Ken Jones is a certified Physician Life Development Coach and an ordained pastor. In addition to his pastoral coaching responsibilities, in 2005 he began serving as the San Francisco Bay Area/Redding Director for the Christian Medical and Dental Associations (CMDA). In January of 2015, he was named Director of Coach Training for CMDA, with responsibilities specifically directed toward training and coaching physicians, dentists, and healthcare executives and administrators. He holds coaching credentials with the International Coach Federation as a professional certified coach (PCC).

Before joining CMDA, Ken and his wife, Randee, pastored several churches. He is a former Writer-in-Residence at Bethany University. His articles on parenting, family, and personal life have appeared in dozens of Christian magazines and periodicals. He is a contributing author for a best-selling book series for teens published by Thomas Nelson, and is the author of three other books. Ken is a recipient of the "Writer of the Year" award at the Mount Hermon Christian Writers Conference in Mount Hermon, California. He is an accomplished musician, and his musical compositions have been published and performed by numerous artists, including Pat Boone.

He has served as a crisis chaplain with the Contra Costa County Sheriff's Office, being honored with the Chaplain of the Year award for that organization. He has taught courses on coaching, writing for publication, storytelling, journaling and devotional life development at Christian writers' workshops and conferences throughout the United States and in Canada and Europe.

Ken is a graduate of Bethany University and has done post graduate studies at both Fuller Seminary and Western Theological Seminary, with emphasis in life coaching. He and his wife, Randee, were married in 1968, and have three sons, and six grandchildren, who are the joy of their lives. Ken enjoys travel, reading, and following baseball, especially the St. Louis Cardinals.

94405355R00088

Made in the USA
San Bernardino, CA
12 November 2018